MAGA in Context

The Rise, Rhetoric, and Reality of a Movement

Justin T. Hileman

Copyright © 2025 by Justin T. Hileman

All rights reserved.

No portion of this book may be reproduced in any form without written permission from the publisher or author, except as permitted by U.S. copyright law.

This publication is designed to provide accurate and authoritative information in regard to the subject matter covered. It is sold with the understanding that neither the author nor the publisher is engaged in rendering legal, investment, accounting or other professional services. While the publisher and author have used their best efforts in preparing this book, they make no representations or warranties with respect to the accuracy or completeness of the contents of this book and specifically disclaim any implied warranties of merchantability or fitness for a particular purpose. No warranty may be created or extended by sales representatives or written sales materials. The advice and strategies contained herein may not be suitable for your situation. You should consult with a professional when appropriate. Neither the publisher nor the author shall be liable for any loss of profit or any other commercial damages, including but not limited to special, incidental, consequential, personal, or other damages.

Contents

Introduction   1

Part 1: The Rise of MAGA   4

1. The Political and Economic Roots of MAGA   5
    The Decline of American Manufacturing and Working-Class Struggles
    The Effects of Globalization, Automation, and the Rise of Anti-Establishment Sentiment
    Post-Reagan Conservatism and the Republican Party's Identity Crisis
    Key takeaways

2. The Tea Party and the Prelude to Trump   16
    The 2008 Financial Crisis and the Rise of Economic Populism
    The Tea Party's Opposition to Obama and Racial Resentment
    Key takeaways

3. Trump's Political Ascent   27
    Trump's Branding as an Anti-Establishment Outsider
    The Role of Right-Wing Media in Elevating Trump
    How Trump Tapped into Racial, Economic, and Cultural Anxieties

    Trump's Ability to Survive Scandals and Reinforce His Brand
    Key takeaways

Part 2: The Rhetoric of MAGA—Appeal vs. Reality   38

4. "Make America Great Again"   39
    The Implied Past America MAGA Longs For—Who Benefited, Who Did not?
    How Historical Context Complicates the Idea of a "Better Past"
    The Danger of Nostalgic Nationalism
    Key takeaways

5. The "Deep State" and Distrust in Institutions   50
    How Trump Weaponized Distrust in Government and the Media
    The Role of Right-Wing Media in Eroding Trust
    The Erosion of Faith in Democracy and Expert Knowledge
    Key takeaways

6. The "America First" Illusion   63
    The Myth of Economic Nationalism: Trade Wars and Their Consequences
    The Reality of Immigration and the U.S. Economy
    The Crime and Public Safety Myth
    Family Separations and the Human Cost of "America First"
    The False Promise of Economic Isolationism
    Key takeaways

7. The Culture War as a Political Strategy   76
    The Role of Grievance Politics in Uniting MAGA's Base
    Misinformation and the Manufactured Panic Over "Wokeism"

The "War on Religion" and Christian Nationalism
How Cultural Anxieties Distract from Economic Concerns
The Myth of Leftist Indoctrination in Public Schools
Key takeaways

Part 3: Debunking the Decontextualized Arguments of MAGA — 90

8. The Economy Under Trump vs. Biden — 91
Claim: "Biden Caused Inflation"
Claim: "Trump Had a Booming Economy Before COVID-19"
Claim: "Biden's Economy Is a Disaster"
Key takeaways

9. Immigration — 107
Claim: "Obama Deported More People Than Trump"
Claim: "Biden Has Open Borders"
Claim: "Immigrants Take American Jobs"
Key takeaways

10. Law and Order — 121
Claim: "Crime Skyrocketed Under Biden"
Claim: "Democrats Want to Defund the Police"
Claim: "Crime Is a Problem in Democrat-Run Cities"
Key takeaways

11. Election Fraud and the Big Lie — 136
Claim: "The 2020 Election Was Stolen"
Claim: "The Media Is Covering Up the Fraud"
The Ongoing Impact on American Democracy
Key takeaways

12. Foreign Policy — 150

Claim: "Trump Started No New Wars"
Claim: "Trump Was Tough on China"
Claim: " Trump Strengthened America's Global Standing"
Key takeaways

Part 4: Reclaiming the Narrative—How Democrats Can Win in a MAGA World — 169

13. A Better Vision for America — 170
    A Vision for Economic Justice: Addressing Inequality and Creating Opportunity
    Rebuilding the Middle Class
    A Vision for Social Justice: Fighting for Racial, Gender, and LGBTQ+ Equality
    Fighting for Racial Justice
    A Vision for Responsible Immigration: Lawful Pathways and Fair Enforcement
    A Vision for National Unity: Building a Politics of Hope, Not Fear
    Strengthening Democracy and Electoral Integrity
    A National Narrative of Shared Purpose
    Key takeaways

14. Fighting Misinformation and Engaging with MAGA Supporters — 208
    The Role of Misinformation in MAGA's Success
    The Big Lie and Election Fraud Claims
    Conspiracy Theories and Fearmongering
    Fighting Misinformation: Restoring Trust in Facts
    Promoting Media Literacy and Critical Thinking
    Strengthening Fact-Checking and Independent Journalism

    Engaging with MAGA Supporters: Moving Beyond the Divide
    Listening to Understand, Not to Argue
    Offering a Unifying Vision
    Leading by Example: Reclaiming the Narrative
    Key takeaways

Conclusion	226
Glossary of Key Political Terms and Acronyms	229
References	232
About the author	257

Introduction

Why Context Matters

The rise of the MAGA movement has profoundly reshaped the political landscape. It thrives on powerful rhetoric and emotional appeals that cut through the noise of everyday political discourse. However, many of its arguments follow a troubling pattern: they strip away essential context, leading to an oversimplified and often distorted version of reality. In an era where misinformation spreads rapidly, understanding and presenting the full context of political issues is more important than ever.

Misinformation and oversimplification are widespread in modern politics. In today's media environment, where soundbites and memes often carry more weight than thorough analysis, ideological echo chambers have become increasingly common. This phenomenon, known as epistemic closure, occurs when individuals or groups become so immersed in their ideological bubbles that they no longer seek out—or even consider—alternative perspectives. The result is intellectual isolation, where the only "truth" that feels credible is the one that reinforces existing beliefs. Within these closed spaces, misinformation thrives.

The internet, social media, and certain media outlets have all contributed to the growth of these ideological silos. They amplify voices that support the MAGA narrative while dismissing opposing viewpoints as "fake news" or parts of a broader conspiracy. In this environment, political movements like MAGA flourish by promoting ideas that resonate emotionally with their followers, even when those ideas are built on misleading or selective interpretations of facts.

This book aims to confront that reality. It offers not just an analysis of the MAGA movement but also a call to restore the missing context in today's political discourse. Without it, we lose sight of the larger truths that shape our society. While the MAGA movement clearly appeals to many, it often distorts reality to fit a narrow and sometimes harmful narrative. Its attacks on Democrats and the broader progressive agenda frequently present a version of history and politics that is incomplete, selective, and designed more to provoke emotional reactions than to encourage informed debate.

Each chapter of this book unpacks these distorted arguments by offering the historical, economic, and social context that is too often overlooked. For example, when MAGA claims that "Biden caused inflation," it ignores global factors like supply chain disruptions and corporate profiteering, which have played a much larger role than any single U.S. policy. Similarly, when the movement insists that "Trump had a booming economy before COVID-19," it overlooks the fact that economic growth was already underway during Obama's presidency, and that Trump's tax cuts disproportionately benefited the wealthy while offering little long-term gain for the middle class. By restoring this missing context, we can work toward building a more accurate and complete understanding of recent history.

This discussion is necessary not just to challenge MAGA's claims, but to provide a broader framework for understanding why those claims resonate. The appeal of MAGA is undeniable—it speaks to the frustrations and fears of many Americans who feel left behind by a rapidly changing world. But it does so by selectively interpreting history and current events to fit a particular worldview. By examining these arguments closely, we can expose how they often obscure deeper, more complex issues.

Understanding the rise of MAGA, the rhetoric that fuels it, and the context it omits is crucial for anyone concerned about the future of American democracy. The stakes are high. If misleading narratives go unchallenged, we risk further eroding trust in our institutions. If misinformation remains unchecked, we risk deepening political polarization and division. But by reclaiming the narrative, we can begin to repair the fractures in our political system and promote a more informed and constructive dialogue.

The issues raised by the MAGA movement—on the economy, immigration, crime, foreign policy, and more—are anything but simple. They are complex, multi-layered problems that demand more than the simplistic solutions often proposed by the movement. This book shows that when we move beyond emotional rhetoric and examine these issues in their full context, the path to real solutions becomes clearer. Most importantly, we can reclaim the conversation about America's future in a way that is grounded in truth, not distortion.

In the chapters ahead, we will examine how key MAGA arguments have been decontextualized and distorted, and how Democrats—and progressives more broadly—can reclaim the conversation. This effort goes beyond debunking false claims. It is about offering a deeper, more nuanced understanding of the forces shaping our political environment. By doing so, we can help build a healthier, better-informed democracy—one where truth matters more than ideological convenience, and where the complexity of our shared challenges is fully acknowledged and addressed.

PART 01

THE RISE OF MAGA

Chapter One
The Political and Economic Roots of MAGA

The emergence of the MAGA movement cannot be understood without examining the political and economic forces that shaped it. Its rise is rooted in long-standing grievances over the decline of American manufacturing, the effects of globalization and automation, and a Republican Party grappling with an identity crisis after the Reagan era. The anger and disillusionment that fueled MAGA were not sudden—they were the result of decades of economic hardship, shifting political dynamics, and a growing sense of alienation among working-class Americans.

The Decline of American Manufacturing and Working-Class Struggles

A central grievance that MAGA effectively tapped into was the belief that America's economic decline, particularly in manufacturing, stemmed from poor trade policies and political neglect. Throughout the 20th century, manufacturing formed the backbone of the American middle class. In the decades following World War II, American industry boomed, providing stable, well-paying jobs that enabled millions to achieve financial security. This postwar prosperity resulted from industrial output and deliberate policy choices, such as labor protections, infrastructure investment, and strong unions, that ensured fair wages and benefits. These policies, combined with rising domestic and international demand, made American workers among the most productive in the world. However, that foundation eroded by the late 20th and early 21st centuries.

Between 2000 and 2010, the United States lost more than 5 million manufacturing jobs (Bureau of Labor Statistics [BLS], 2021). This decline was driven by several factors, including automation, globalization, and trade agreements that made outsourcing cheaper for corporations. The North American Free Trade Agreement (NAFTA), signed in 1994, and China's entry into the World Trade Organization (WTO) in 2001 accelerated the offshoring of U.S. manufacturing, causing profound economic disruption in industrial regions (Autor et al., 2016). For many, this marked the start of a painful economic shift that left communities in Pennsylvania, Ohio, and Michigan especially vulnerable. These states bore the brunt of deindustrialization, as once-thriving industrial cities and towns hollowed out and job opportunities vanished, fostering a deep sense of abandonment. Once home to robust blue-collar communities, these areas would become key battlegrounds in the rise of MAGA.

While free trade agreements brought cheaper consumer goods and growth in some sectors, they devastated traditional manufacturing hubs, leaving a generation of workers struggling to find comparable employment. Economic theory suggests that free trade benefits all parties in the long run. However, the short-term pain of job displacement in industries like steel, textiles, and automotive manufacturing was often ignored. As corporations moved operations overseas, they did not just outsource jobs—they gutted entire communities. Once-vibrant industrial towns became hollowed out, plagued by rising poverty, drug addiction, and despair.

A 2016 study found that the "China Shock"—the period following China's 2001 WTO accession, which triggered a surge in Chinese exports and a spike in U.S. imports—caused long-term job losses in American manufacturing hubs, with little evidence that displaced workers successfully transitioned to new industries (Autor et al., 2016). This economic displacement bred widespread resentment, which Donald Trump later harnessed through populist rhetoric that blamed global elites and bad trade deals for job losses. His message resonated most strongly in the towns hit hardest by manufacturing's decline, offering a critique of trade policy and a reflection of more profound cultural dislocation.

MAGA's success was built on the anger of voters who felt betrayed by a system that once promised prosperity through hard work, but instead delivered obsolescence.

The loss of manufacturing jobs was not just an economic issue but a cultural blow. It eroded the sense of identity many Americans had tied to jobs that once provided dignity and stability. In regions where factories had been the lifeblood of communities, the collapse of manufacturing felt like a betrayal of core American values. This pain was compounded by the slow and often ineffective responses from political elites, who offered few concrete solutions beyond vague promises about retraining workers or investing in emerging technologies—proposals seen as distant hopes rather than immediate remedies.

In this context, MAGA was not only responding to economic grievances but also to emotional ones. The slogan "Make America Great Again" resonated because it voiced a perceived loss of something fundamental: belief in the American Dream—the idea that anyone willing to work hard could achieve prosperity. MAGA supporters, especially those in former manufacturing hubs, were not merely seeking jobs; they were seeking the restoration of dignity and the reclaiming of a future that had come to feel increasingly out of reach. The rise of populism was, in many ways, a direct response to the economic and social forces that had eroded working-class livelihoods. It reflected a collective yearning to return to a past many felt had been stolen.

The Effects of Globalization, Automation, and the Rise of Anti-Establishment Sentiment

Globalization was not the only driver behind the decline in American manufacturing jobs—automation also played a crucial role. Advances in robotics and artificial intelligence have significantly reduced the need for human labor across many industries, resulting in job losses even where production remains domestic. Automation introduced more efficient production methods, but it also displaced many workers. According to a study by Acemoglu and Restrepo (2020), each new industrial robot led to an estimated loss of 3.3 jobs in local labor markets. Despite this, politicians, particularly within the MAGA movement, seldom acknowledged automation as a significant factor in job loss. Instead, they focused almost exclusively on trade and immigration. This omission is telling. Automation's transformative role in reshaping the labor market presents complex questions about the future of work—questions many political leaders have avoided. By sidestepping these issues, they failed to engage with the broader implications of technological change, offering instead simplified narratives that placed blame on external forces.

The economic pain caused by these structural changes was not evenly distributed. Rural and industrial communities were hit hardest, while coastal cities and tech hubs often experienced growth, widening regional inequalities. This imbalance fueled a growing sense of alienation and resentment among working-class Americans, mainly white workers without college degrees. A study by Case and Deaton (2020) found that economic decline in these regions correlated with rising rates of "deaths of despair"—suicides, drug overdoses, and alcohol-related illnesses—highlighting the profound societal toll of economic stagnation. The erosion of opportunity in these areas was more than a matter of lost jobs; it led to a broader sense of hopelessness and social fragmentation. Communities that had once relied on factory jobs and stable industries now grappled with the fallout of economic shifts they felt powerless to control.

Midlife mortality from "deaths of despair" across countries

Men and women ages 50-54, deaths by drugs, alcohol, and suicide

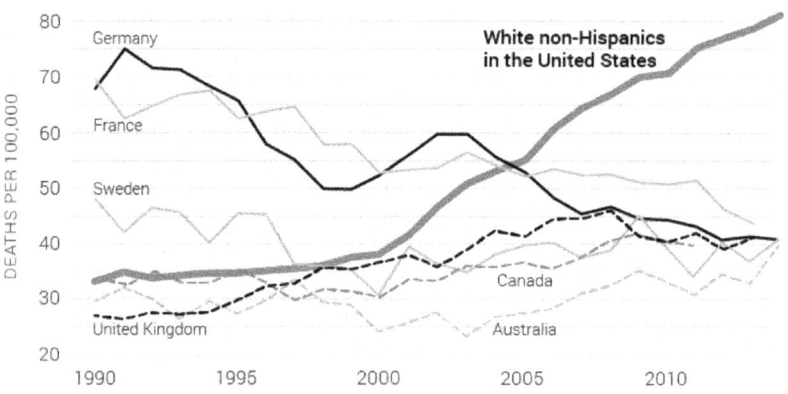

Source: "Mortality and morbidity in the 21st century" by Anne Case and Angus Deaton, Brookings Papers on Economic Activity, Spring 2017.

Working class white Americans are now dying in middle age at faster rates than minority groups

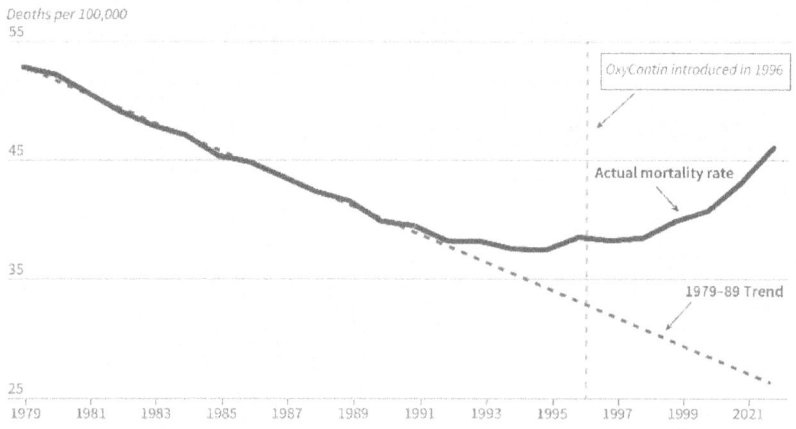

Mortality Rates from 'Deaths of Despair': Whites Aged 45-64

Deaths of despair include deaths due to suicide, poisoning, or liver disease.
Source: Researchers' calculations using data from the CDC

Trump's 2016 campaign capitalized on this frustration by promising to bring back manufacturing jobs and punish companies that outsourced production. His message resonated with voters who felt ignored by both major parties, especially by establishment Republicans who had long supported free trade and globalization. Trump's appeal was rooted in nostalgia for a perceived golden age of American manufacturing. Still, it also reflected a desire to reclaim agency—a belief that voters could regain control over their economic futures. While his policies, such as tariffs on Chinese goods, had mixed economic effects (Bown, 2020), the symbolic power of his rhetoric was undeniable. For many, the appeal lay less in the technical specifics of trade policy and more in the promise of restoring national pride and self-determination—values they believed had been lost during decades of deindustrialization and technological change.

A deep distrust of experts, media, and academic institutions intensified this alienation. Economic hardship and stagnant upward mobility fueled growing skepticism toward traditional sources of authority. As people began to feel that existing systems no longer served their interests, many turned to alternative explanations that offered more immediate and emotionally satisfying answers. MAGA supporters often gravitated toward conspiracy theories that provided simplified narratives, blaming economic decline on shadowy elites, deep-state actors, or globalist agendas rather than acknowledging technological change or structural economic shifts (Hofstadter, 1964). These beliefs reinforced an "us versus them" mindset, in which ordinary citizens were seen as victims of powerful, unseen forces working to undermine their way of life.

This skepticism toward mainstream media, science, and academia fueled a rise in anti-intellectual sentiment. Universities and research institutions were increasingly portrayed as corrupt entities aligned with liberal elites. Though rooted in fear and frustration, this narrative played a crucial role in shaping MAGA's appeal. It offered a worldview in which elite institutions had failed, and the working class, long overlooked, was framed as the actual, unrecognized engine of the nation.

Post-Reagan Conservatism and the Republican Party's Identity Crisis

The economic grievances that fueled MAGA were not solely the result of global trade and automation; internal shifts within the Republican Party also shaped them. Throughout the late 20th century, the GOP increasingly aligned itself with pro-business, free-market policies that often prioritized corporate interests over the concerns of the working class. The Reagan Revolution of the 1980s cemented this direction, emphasizing tax cuts, deregulation, and a reduced role for government in the economy (Skowronek, 2011). Neoliberalism—an economic philosophy advocating free markets, privatization, and minimal government intervention—became the party's guiding framework.

Reagan's message that "government is the problem" resonated with many voters, offering a vision of limited government and economic freedom that promised to unleash American entrepreneurship. However, the emphasis on market-driven solutions often came at the expense of the working class. These policies facilitated wealth accumulation among the wealthy and large corporations while leaving many ordinary Americans to navigate an increasingly volatile economy. The party's ideological shift toward neoliberalism not only reshaped Republican policy but also planted the seeds of a broader identity crisis.

For a time, this approach proved politically successful. Economic growth in the 1980s and 1990s, particularly during President Bill Clinton's tenure, created a sense of prosperity that masked deeper structural problems.

However, by the early 2000s, cracks in the foundation began to appear. The 2008 financial crisis significantly affected the credibility of free-market conservatism. As millions of Americans lost their jobs and homes while major financial institutions received government bailouts, the contrast between Wall Street's rescue and Main Street's suffering deepened public disillusionment.

This stark disparity fueled a growing sense of betrayal and exposed the limitations of deregulated capitalism. Many working-class voters—especially in rural and industrial communities—felt abandoned by both parties. This discontent fed into the rising anti-establishment sentiment that would later become central to the MAGA movement. The GOP's long-standing embrace of big business and free-market orthodoxy, once central to its identity, increasingly appeared out of touch with the needs of the voters it sought to represent, particularly those whose livelihoods had been devastated by globalization and automation.

The Tea Party movement, which emerged in response to the economic crisis and the election of Barack Obama, signaled the beginning of a more profound ideological rift within the Republican Party. Although the movement initially focused on opposing government spending and the Affordable Care Act, it also tapped into broader anti-establishment sentiment. Its populist rhetoric—with calls to "take back our country" and disdain for political elites—resonated with many Americans who felt alienated by the political establishment. The movement shifted from traditional conservatism toward a more populist brand that rejected Washington's elite consensus.

This shift paved the way for Trump's rise. He positioned himself as an outsider willing to break from Republican orthodoxy. Unlike previous GOP leaders, he openly rejected free trade agreements, criticized corporate outsourcing, and promised to restore economic security for the working class—stances that resonated with voters who felt left behind by both parties (Skocpol & Williamson, 2016). Trump's rhetoric, which cast him as a champion of the forgotten working class, represented a sharp break from the neoliberal policies that had dominated the GOP for decades. His appeal lay in his ability to channel the disillusionment of voters who had watched their communities decline while global elites thrived.

The political and economic roots of MAGA run deep. The decline of American manufacturing, the disruptive effects of globalization and automation, and a Republican Party increasingly disconnected from its working-class base all contributed to the movement's rise. These forces created frustration and disillusionment, which Trump effectively exploited in his 2016 campaign. The GOP's transformation from a party of economic conservatism to one of populist nationalism set the stage for MAGA's ascent. Trump's success reflected, in part, the party's failure to respond to the evolving needs of working-class voters, many of whom felt abandoned by the very institution that had once claimed to represent them.

Understanding these roots is essential to understanding MAGA itself. Addressing these concerns will require political reform and a broader effort to rebuild trust in expertise, government, and the economic future of working-class America.

Key takeaways

- MAGA's rise is rooted in decades of economic decline and industrial job losses, especially in the Rust Belt.

- Globalization and automation were key drivers of working-class displacement, though often underplayed in MAGA rhetoric.

- Trump tapped into feelings of betrayal and disillusionment, promising to restore economic dignity.

- The GOP's shift toward neoliberalism alienated its working-class base, paving the way for populist nationalism.

CHAPTER TWO
The Tea Party and the Prelude to Trump

The political forces that led to the rise of Donald Trump and the MAGA movement were not sudden developments but the culmination of years of discontent, resentment, and shifting conservative ideology. The seeds of Trumpism were planted long before his 2016 campaign, nurtured by deep mistrust of government, economic anxiety, and a growing rift between establishment Republicans and their base. Nowhere was this transformation more evident than in the rise of the Tea Party movement, which burst onto the political scene in the wake of the 2008 financial crisis. What began as a revolt against government overreach quickly evolved into a powerful force that reshaped the Republican Party, inflamed racial and cultural tensions, and laid the groundwork for the populist nationalism that would later define Trump's presidency. To understand MAGA, one must first understand the Tea Party—the movement that made it possible.

The 2008 Financial Crisis and the Rise of Economic Populism

The Tea Party emerged after the 2008 financial crisis—a period marked by economic uncertainty and widespread anger at both the government and Wall Street. The crisis, triggered by the subprime mortgage market's collapse, led to the worst economic downturn since the Great Depression. Unemployment soared, home values plummeted, and millions of Americans faced foreclosure (Mian & Sufi, 2014). The rapid collapse shattered public trust in financial institutions and the federal government's ability to protect the middle class. Many voters felt betrayed, believing that the very institutions meant to ensure fairness and economic stability had instead been complicit in their suffering. This sense of betrayal helped lay the foundation for the rise of populist sentiment.

A key factor in the crisis was the deregulation of the financial industry, most notably, the repeal of the Glass-Steagall Act. Initially passed in 1933, Glass-Steagall was enacted in response to the banking failures of the Great Depression, which had been fueled by speculative investments made by banks holding ordinary Americans' deposits. The law separated commercial banking (focused on deposits and loans) from investment banking (which engaged in higher-risk activities such as trading and securities underwriting). This separation created a firewall that prevented banks from using federally insured deposits for speculative trading, thereby reducing the risk of another systemic collapse (Krugman, 2009).

By the late 20th century, however, financial industry lobbyists and many policymakers argued that Glass-Steagall was outdated and hindered competition in a global economy. With bipartisan support, the law was repealed in 1999 through the Gramm-Leach-Bliley Act, signed into law by President Bill Clinton. This repeal allowed commercial and investment banks to merge, creating massive financial conglomerates such as Citigroup, JPMorgan Chase, and Bank of America—institutions that engaged in traditional banking and high-risk speculative trading. Without the protections of Glass-Steagall, these firms aggressively expanded into the mortgage-backed securities market, securitizing risky subprime loans into financial products that would later implode during the 2008 crash (Stiglitz, 2010).

Critics of the repeal argued that it encouraged reckless behavior by allowing banks to take excessive risks with customer deposits. This led to the creation of complex financial products like collateralized debt obligations (CDOs) and credit default swaps (CDSs), amplifying the damage caused by the subprime mortgage crisis. Deregulation allowed large banks to engage in risky lending practices under the assumption that the federal government would bail them out if things went wrong—a belief that ultimately proved true.

In response, the federal government launched a series of bailouts to stabilize the financial system, most notably the Troubled Asset Relief Program (TARP), which allocated $700 billion to rescue banks deemed "too big to fail" (Congressional Budget Office, 2012). While these measures were credited with preventing a total economic collapse, they were deeply unpopular, especially among conservatives who viewed them as excessive government intervention and evidence of a corrupt alliance between Washington and Wall Street. This moment marked the beginning of a populist backlash, fueled by the belief that the government's actions disproportionately benefited financial elites while ordinary citizens were left to bear the consequences.

A defining feature of the Tea Party's rise was its ability to frame government intervention as a direct attack on the working class in favor of elites and corporations. Many adherents believed the federal bailouts prioritized wealthy bankers and financial executives while ignoring the struggles of everyday Americans. This economic populism—pitting the "real" American worker against Washington and Wall Street—became a central theme in Donald Trump's later campaign rhetoric. It was a narrative of "us versus them," in which elites were seen as living in an entirely different reality, insulated from the hardships faced by working-class communities. By casting economic relief efforts as betrayals, the Tea Party successfully mobilized widespread discontent, particularly among those who felt left behind in a rapidly changing economy.

This anger crystallized in early 2009 when CNBC commentator Rick Santelli delivered a now-famous rant on live television. Standing on the floor of the Chicago Mercantile Exchange, Santelli denounced government intervention in the economy, especially mortgage bailouts, and exclaimed:

> *"This is America! How many of you people want to pay for Your neighbor's mortgage that has an extra bathroom and can't pay their bills?*
> *Raise your hand! ... We're thinking of having a Chicago Tea Party in July.*
> *All you capitalists that want to show up to Lake Michigan, I'm gonna start organizing it."*

Santelli's impassioned speech tapped into growing frustration among conservatives, many of whom believed government bailouts rewarded irresponsibility while hardworking Americans were left behind. His call for a "Tea Party" struck a chord across conservative media. Within months, grassroots activists adopted the name, organizing protests against the bailouts, government spending, and eventually, President Obama's signature policy achievement—the Affordable Care Act (Skocpol & Williamson, 2016). This early outrage framed the Tea Party as a movement opposed to both big government and economic elitism, positioning itself as the voice of the "real" American taxpayer.

However, the movement's messaging was often contradictory. While Tea Party activists denounced government spending, many regions that showed the most substantial support for the movement also relied heavily on federal assistance programs. This contradiction revealed deeper, more emotional grievances—resentment toward perceived undeserving recipients of government aid, distrust of Washington elites, and anxiety over the country's shifting demographics. The Tea Party's vocal opposition to "entitlements" often ignored the fact that many of its supporters benefited from programs such as Social Security, Medicare, and farm subsidies. This tension reflected a broader emotional undercurrent: a yearning for a nostalgic vision of America, where hard work and personal responsibility were seen as the primary paths to success.

Moreover, the Tea Party's initial focus on fiscal conservatism and limited government soon became more complex and divisive. What began as an economically driven movement quickly became entangled with issues of race, immigration, and cultural identity. The election of Barack Obama, the nation's first Black president, was seen by many Tea Party members as a sign of a changing America—one no longer dominated by white, working-class voters. This racial anxiety was often expressed as a cultural crisis, with many in the Tea Party viewing Obama's presidency as symbolic of a shift toward a more diverse, progressive, and government-dependent society. These anxieties would later surface in Donald Trump's rhetoric, as he tapped into fears about demographic change and national identity, making him a natural heir to the Tea Party's political legacy.

The Tea Party's transformation from an economic populist movement into a culturally charged political force set the stage for Trump's rise. His campaign—built on the Tea Party's foundations of anti-government populism, nationalist rhetoric, and economic frustration—was a direct extension of the anger and disillusionment that had been building since the 2008 crisis. Just as the Tea Party arose in response to the perceived failures of government and political elites, Trump positioned himself as the ultimate outsider who could restore America's greatness by dismantling the institutions the Tea Party had long opposed.

The Tea Party's Opposition to Obama and Racial Resentment

Although the Tea Party framed its opposition in economic terms, research suggests that its rapid rise was also significantly influenced by racial anxieties and cultural backlash following the election of America's first Black president. In a 2013 study, political scientists Matt A. Barreto and Christopher S. Parker analyzed the motivations behind Tea Party support and found that racial resentment was a significant predictor. Many adherents viewed President Barack Obama as an illegitimate leader, reflecting deeper fears about America's shifting demographics. This sentiment was tied to a broader perception that the country was changing in ways that alienated them, fueling a reactionary movement grounded in the belief that America had declined. Their research underscores how economic concerns among Tea Party supporters were often intertwined with fears about demographic change and the perceived erosion of traditional American—implicitly white—identity. The Tea Party's rhetoric frequently centered on the idea that "real Americans" were losing their country, a narrative that resonated with a base that felt increasingly sidelined by liberal, multicultural, and diverse coalitions.

One of the clearest examples of this racialized opposition was the birther movement, which falsely claimed that Obama was not born in the United States and was therefore ineligible to be president. This conspiracy theory, which Donald Trump would later champion, was not confined to the political fringe; it was widely embraced within the Tea Party. A 2011 poll found that 47% of Tea Party supporters believed Obama was not born in the U.S., compared to 23% of the general public (Pew Research Center, 2011). Birtherism was not simply a challenge to a political opponent's credentials—it reflected a broader refusal to accept that a Black man could rightfully hold the nation's highest office. This attack on Obama's legitimacy echoed historical efforts to undermine Black political power, invoking longstanding narratives that cast Black leaders as unqualified or fundamentally un-American. By embracing birtherism, Tea Party activists and conservative media figures reinforced a tradition of racialized fearmongering that portrayed nonwhite political figures as threats to the existing order.

Where Was Barack Obama Born?

	In the United States %	In another country %	DK %
Total	55	23	22=100
Staunch Conservs	24	47	29=100
Main Street Reps	34	35	31=100
Libertarians	45	19	36=100
Disaffecteds	37	34	29=100
Post-Moderns	71	9	20=100
New Coalition Dems	66	24	10=100
Hard-Pressed Dems	56	21	24=100
Solid Liberals	95	*	5=100

PEW RESEARCH CENTER 2011 Political Typology.
QCB6. Figures may not add to 100% because of rounding.

Source: CBS News. (2010, April 14). *CBS News/New York Times Poll: Tea Party Movement.* CBS News. Public opinion on the attention given to African American issues, comparing responses from Tea Party, Non-Tea Party, All Americans, and White respondents, highlighting differing views on whether the attention is too much, about right, or too little.

Beyond birtherism, the Tea Party's policy positions often carried racial undertones. Opposition to the Affordable Care Act (ACA), for example, was frequently framed as resistance to a government "handout" that disproportionately benefited minorities, even though the ACA expanded healthcare access for Americans of all racial backgrounds (Tesler, 2016).

Conservative media and Tea Party rhetoric often described the ACA as "reparations" or a giveaway to "takers," invoking the long-standing racial stereotype that government assistance primarily benefits Black and Latino communities at the expense of hardworking white taxpayers. This racialized framing of public programs fit into a broader conservative narrative that associated welfare and government aid with racial minorities, reinforcing persistent grievances among white working- and middle-class voters. Similar tropes had been deployed in earlier decades, most notably in Ronald Reagan's references to "welfare queens" in the 1980s—a rhetorical strategy designed to stoke resentment by suggesting that tax dollars were being unfairly redistributed to undeserving minorities.

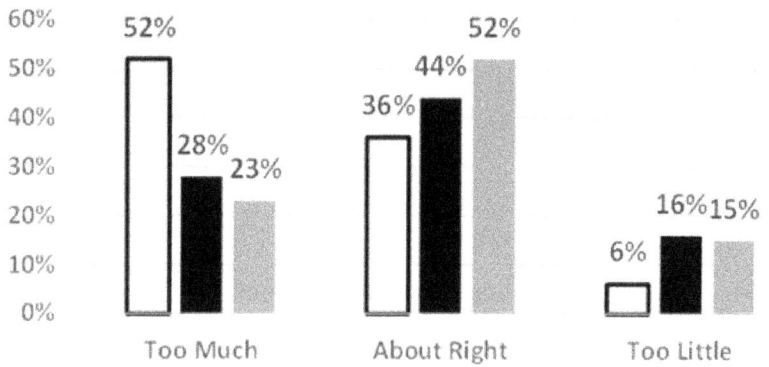

Source: CBS News. (2010, April 14). *CBS News/New York Times Poll: Tea Party Movement.* CBS News. Public opinion on the attention given to African American issues, comparing responses from Tea Party, Non-Tea Party, All Americans, and White respondents, highlighting differing views on whether the attention is too much, about right, or too little.

Further evidence of racial resentment within the Tea Party can be found in research by Knowles, Lowery, and Schaumberg (2010), which showed that racial attitudes were a significant predictor of opposition to Obama and his policies, even when controlling for ideological and economic factors. Similarly, Feldman (2014) found that Tea Party supporters were more likely to agree with statements reflecting racial resentment, such as the belief that African Americans receive unfair advantages in society. The persistence of these beliefs underscores that the movement's grievances were not solely about economic hardship or government overreach, but also about who was perceived to be benefiting from government policies. The Tea Party's ability to channel racial resentment into political action foreshadowed the way Trump's campaign would later do the same, blaming immigration, multiculturalism, and political correctness for the perceived economic and cultural decline of "real America."

The Tea Party's opposition to Obama, rooted in both economic and racial anxieties, created a deep well of resentment that Trump would later tap into. Although the Tea Party faded as an organized movement, its influence endures in the MAGA era. Many of the same themes that defined the Tea Party—distrust of government, hostility toward progressive social policies, and racialized fear of demographic change—became even more pronounced under Trump. His ability to mobilize these grievances to consolidate conservative support was not a break from Republican tradition but a continuation and intensification of long-developing trends.

The grievances that fueled the Tea Party—economic frustration, cultural anxiety, and deep distrust of government—remain central to conservative politics today. These forces have not disappeared; they have been repackaged and amplified under Trump's leadership. What began as opposition to Obama's presidency evolved into a broader rejection of the political establishment, the media, and any institution perceived to promote progressive values. The Tea Party helped foster a political environment where fact-based policy debates gave way to identity-driven grievances, clearing the path for figures like Trump to thrive.

The persistence of these dynamics suggests that the political and cultural battles ignited during the Tea Party era are far from over. They continue to shape American politics and public discourse. The shift toward grievance-driven, populist conservatism, where opposition to demographic change and social reform is framed as a defense of traditional American values, has become the dominant force in right-wing politics, ensuring that the legacy of the Tea Party lives on through the MAGA movement.

Key takeaways

- The Tea Party movement emerged from backlash to the 2008 financial crisis and government bailouts.

- It fused economic populism with cultural and racial resentment, especially following Obama's election.

- Contradictions in Tea Party messaging revealed deeper anxieties about changing American identity.

- The movement laid the foundation for Trump's anti-establishment and racially charged political style.

Chapter Three
Trump's Political Ascent

Donald Trump's rise from real estate mogul and reality television star to the most influential figure in the Republican Party was no accident—it was the culmination of deep-seated economic, racial, and cultural anxieties that had been brewing for decades. While the Tea Party laid the groundwork for his success, Trump's unique ability to exploit existing frustrations, weaponize right-wing media, and present himself as an anti-establishment outsider made his ascent possible. Understanding how he leveraged these dynamics is essential to understanding the broader MAGA movement.

Trump's Branding as an Anti-Establishment Outsider

Donald Trump's public persona was shaped over decades through his business ventures, media appearances, and most notably, his time as host of The Apprentice. To many Americans, he embodied the ultimate success story—a self-made billionaire who knew how to "win" in business and, by extension, in politics (Fraser, 2015). Although this image was primarily built on exaggeration and myth, it became central to his appeal when he launched his presidential campaign in 2015. Trump repeatedly touted his business acumen, contrasting himself with career politicians, whom he painted as incompetent, corrupt, and beholden to special interests. His ability to present himself as a political outsider with real-world experience made him an attractive alternative to establishment Republicans who had lost credibility with their base.

Unlike traditional politicians, Trump embraced a brash, unfiltered style that resonated with voters disillusioned by party elites. He cast himself as a straight-talker who "told it like it is" and was not afraid to challenge political correctness, which had become associated with liberal cultural dominance in conservative circles (Sides, Tesler, & Vavreck, 2018). By tapping into conservative grievances over free speech, media bias, and the so-called liberal elite, he positioned himself as a warrior against the forces many on the right believed were eroding American culture.

In stark contrast, Hillary Clinton's 2016 campaign followed a conventional political playbook, emphasizing experience and continuity. Having served as First Lady, U.S. Senator, and Secretary of State, Clinton highlighted her public service record as proof of her leadership readiness. However, her long tenure in government also made her a symbol of the establishment that many voters felt had failed to address their concerns.

While many initially dismissed Trump's campaign as a publicity stunt, his outsider status was precisely what many Republican voters sought. After years of perceived betrayal by the party establishment, who had promised to repeal Obamacare, secure the border, and fight for the working class but often failed to deliver, Trump's blunt, uncompromising rhetoric was a welcome change (McAdam & Kloos, 2019). His willingness to defy party orthodoxy on issues like trade and foreign policy further boosted his appeal among voters who felt abandoned by both parties.

Unlike traditional Republicans who championed free trade, Trump openly criticized NAFTA, China's entry into the WTO, and other globalization policies that had harmed American manufacturing. This shift allowed him to win over working-class voters who had previously been skeptical of the GOP, particularly in Rust Belt states hit hard by deindustrialization.

The Role of Right-Wing Media in Elevating Trump

Trump's rise would have been unlikely without the support of right-wing media, which played a crucial role in legitimizing his candidacy and amplifying his message. Fox News, in particular, provided him with a platform long before he announced his presidential run, allowing him to build a loyal following among conservative viewers. He was a frequent guest on Fox News programs, where he shared his political views on immigration, trade, and President Barack Obama. His promotion of birtherism—a conspiracy theory questioning Obama's citizenship—received substantial airtime on Fox, reinforcing doubts about Obama's legitimacy among conservative audiences. This early media exposure helped establish Trump as a political figure within the Republican base well before his official campaign launch.

During the 2016 campaign, Fox News dedicated more coverage to Trump than to any other Republican candidate, often in a favorable light (Hemmer, 2019). Hosts like Sean Hannity and Tucker Carlson regularly defended him against criticism. At the same time, other conservative outlets, such as Breitbart and The Daily Caller, framed his campaign as a grassroots uprising against the political elite. Under Steve Bannon's leadership, Breitbart actively promoted Trump's populist message and helped rally support among nationalist and anti-establishment conservatives. This alliance between Trump and right-wing media was mutually beneficial: Trump delivered sensational, headline-generating content that boosted ratings, while media outlets reinforced his image as the ultimate outsider challenging the establishment.

Beyond traditional media, Trump's mastery of social media—especially Twitter—gave him a direct, unfiltered line to his supporters. Unlike past candidates who relied on campaign spokespeople and press conferences, Trump bypassed traditional media entirely. He used social media to attack opponents, spread misinformation, and rally his base in real time (Ott, 2017). His Twitter account became a central tool for shaping political narratives, setting the day's news cycle, and focusing public attention squarely on him. Through inflammatory remarks, personal attacks, and policy declarations, Trump's ability to dominate social media allowed him to control public discourse like no previous candidate had. Conservative media further amplified his tweets, creating an echo chamber that reinforced his messaging and deepened partisan divisions.

This constant media presence had a profound impact. Research shows that repeated exposure to Trump's messages—even negative ones—helped solidify his dominance in the GOP primary. A study by Boczkowski, Mitchelstein, and Matassi (2018) found that, regardless of tone, Trump's control over the news cycle significantly boosted his visibility and perceived strength as a candidate. Unlike traditional politicians who tried to avoid controversy, Trump embraced it, understanding that even negative press kept him at the center of political conversation. His media strategy was no accident—it was a deliberate approach tailored to a modern news environment that thrives on sensationalism and audience engagement.

How Trump Tapped into Racial, Economic, and Cultural Anxieties

While Trump's economic message, focused on trade protectionism and reviving manufacturing, resonated with working-class voters, his success was also deeply rooted in racial and cultural grievances. He launched his campaign by infamously referring to Mexican immigrants as "rapists" and "criminals," immediately signaling that his candidacy would embrace nativist and nationalist themes (Heer, 2019). This explicit rhetoric marked a departure from previous Republican candidates, who typically relied on subtler racial appeals through coded language, such as Ronald Reagan's reference to "welfare queens" or George H. W. Bush's Willie Horton ad. Trump, by contrast, openly vilified immigrants, Muslims, and communities of color, making racial and cultural scapegoating a central theme of his campaign rather than a subtext.

His promises to build a border wall and implement a "Muslim ban" appealed to voters who viewed immigration as a threat to American culture and economic security (Jardina, 2019). These proposals were more than just policy positions—they were symbolic gestures meant to reassure white voters that he would restore a racial and cultural hierarchy they believed was eroding. By casting immigrants as criminals and job stealers, Trump offered an external enemy to blame for economic decline. This narrative reinforced the belief that white, working-class Americans were victims of a rigged system that favored foreigners and minorities at their expense.

Although economic anxiety was often cited as a key factor in Trump's appeal, research shows that racial resentment, not financial hardship, was his strongest support predictor in 2016 (Sides, Tesler, & Vavreck, 2018). His campaign effectively merged economic frustrations with racialized explanations, blaming job losses on globalization and immigration rather than corporate misconduct or technological disruption. This strategy reflected a long-standing pattern in American politics: in times of economic distress and social change, racial scapegoating tends to intensify.

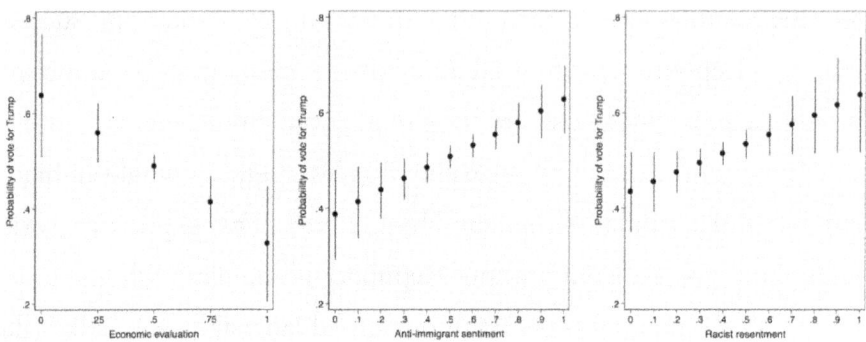

Trump's rhetoric was especially effective among white voters without a college degree. This demographic had been drifting from the Democratic Party for years but had never coalesced so decisively around a single candidate. Many of these voters had once supported Democrats, particularly in union-heavy states like Pennsylvania, Michigan, and Wisconsin. However, they felt increasingly alienated by the party's growing focus on social justice and multiculturalism (Cramer, 2016). His call to "Make America Great Again" resonated because it evoked nostalgia for a time when white, Christian, working-class Americans felt culturally and economically dominant, before globalization, mass immigration, and rising racial diversity reshaped the nation's demographics.

Trump also capitalized on the growing backlash against social progressivism, which had intensified during the Obama years. Issues such as same-sex marriage, transgender rights, and the Black Lives Matter movement had gained national prominence, fueling resentment among conservative voters who felt their traditional values were under siege.

The increasing visibility of social justice movements, combined with demographic shifts that made America less white and more diverse, fueled a sense of cultural displacement among many on the right. Trump's blunt rejection of "political correctness" and his willingness to mock social justice efforts signaled to these voters that he would push back against what they saw as liberal overreach (Gillion, 2020). His attacks on NFL players who kneeled during the national anthem, for example, were not merely about patriotism—they reinforced the notion that Black activism was un-American and that traditional symbols of national unity should remain unquestioned. His rhetoric on crime, often invoking images of inner-city violence, played into longstanding racial stereotypes that associated Blackness with lawlessness. These appeals to cultural resentment helped solidify his support among conservatives who felt alienated by 21st-century social changes.

Even Trump's economic populism carried racial undertones. While he framed his opposition to free trade and his promises to revive American manufacturing as efforts to protect working-class jobs, his messaging overwhelmingly focused on white industrial workers, mainly ignoring the diverse working-class populations of urban centers. His attacks on welfare programs, "globalist" elites, and inner-city crime reinforced the conservative narrative that government aid primarily benefited racial minorities at the expense of white taxpayers. His rhetoric on globalization and outsourcing, instead of critiquing corporate capitalism, often blamed foreign nations and nonwhite workers, promoting the idea that economic struggles stemmed from external threats undermining American greatness. By shifting attention away from structural economic issues and onto racialized scapegoats—immigrants, China, Black Lives Matter activists—Trump offered a clear but misleading explanation for the hardships facing working-class Americans.

Trump's ability to fuse economic grievances with racial and cultural anxieties fundamentally reshaped the Republican Party, making nativism and racial identity politics central to its platform. While previous Republican candidates had appealed to working-class white voters through economic promises and religious conservatism, Trump went further, openly embracing racial grievance as a political strategy. His success demonstrated that an explicitly nationalist, racially charged campaign could be electorally viable, setting a precedent for future GOP candidates. The normalization of anti-immigrant rhetoric, the resurgence of white identity politics, and the demonization of social justice movements became defining features of modern conservatism, ensuring that Trump's influence would extend far beyond his presidency.

The impact of Trump's racial and cultural appeals continues to shape American politics. His use of nationalist slogans like "America First," his attacks on diversity initiatives, and his embrace of conspiracy theories about white victimhood have entrenched racial grievance within conservative discourse. The rise of Trumpism has made it clear that racial and cultural anxieties—not just economic concerns—are key drivers of right-wing populism in the United States. By channeling these anxieties into a powerful political movement, Trump ensured that racial identity politics would remain central to the Republican Party for years to come.

Trump's Ability to Survive Scandals and Reinforce His Brand

Trump's ability to survive scandals that would have ended most political careers was not merely a matter of luck; it stemmed from his skill at controlling the narrative and turning controversy into a rallying cry. From the Access Hollywood tape, where he bragged about sexually assaulting women, to numerous allegations of corruption and dishonesty, Trump faced constant controversy throughout his 2016 campaign. However, rather than being derailed, he used these moments to reinforce his brand as a fighter against the political establishment. Unlike traditional politicians, who might issue formal apologies or withdraw under similar circumstances, Trump doubled down, refusing to admit wrongdoing and attacking his critics' credibility instead.

His strategy was simple but effective: whenever he faced criticism, he cast himself as the victim of a biased media and corrupt elites trying to silence him. This narrative tapped into a long-standing distrust of mainstream institutions among conservative voters (Levitsky & Ziblatt, 2018). By presenting himself as the ultimate outsider, he convinced supporters that attacks on him were, in fact, attacks on them. This dynamic fostered intense loyalty among his base. Each new scandal further proved that he was battling a corrupt system designed to suppress their voices. His ability to turn controversies into referendums on the media, the political elite, and even the democratic process ensured that his core supporters remained unmoved by allegations that would have sunk other politicians.

This dynamic was especially evident in Trump's response to criticism from within his party. When establishment Republicans like Jeb Bush and Mitt Romney denounced him, Trump used their opposition to bolster his outsider status. Instead of seeking unity with the GOP establishment, he went on the offensive, casting traditional Republicans as out-of-touch elites who had betrayed the American people. By positioning himself against Democrats and conservative leaders, Trump forged a new political identity that would later define the MAGA movement: one that rejected not only liberalism but also the Republican old guard, viewed as complicit in the nation's decline (McAdam & Kloos, 2019). His attacks on figures such as the Bush family, John McCain, and Paul Ryan were not just about policy—they were part of a broader effort to rebrand the Republican Party in his image. This scorched-earth approach permanently altered the GOP's power structure, making loyalty to Trump a defining feature of Republican politics.

Another key factor in Trump's resilience was the role of right-wing media in shielding him from political fallout. Outlets like Fox News, Breitbart, and One America News Network consistently framed controversies as smear campaigns orchestrated by the liberal media. This created an alternate information ecosystem in which Trump's scandals were downplayed, reframed as political persecution, or dismissed outright. The normalization of conspiracy theories—such as claims that the Access Hollywood tape was a deep-state plot or that the Russia investigation was a hoax—helped insulate him from accountability. This media strategy reinforced the perception that every attack on Trump was illegitimate, strengthening the belief among his supporters that he alone was standing up to a corrupt establishment.

Trump's rise capitalized on economic frustration, racial and cultural resentment, the growing influence of right-wing media, and widespread disillusionment with both major parties. He did not create these forces but understood how to exploit them like no other politician had. His campaign transformed the Republican Party, shifting it away from traditional conservative ideals and toward a new brand of nationalist, populist politics.

The MAGA movement that emerged from his presidency is not merely about Trump as an individual—it reflects the more profound anxieties and grievances that propelled him to power. More importantly, his ability to survive a scandal has set a new precedent in American politics. It demonstrated that, for a certain kind of populist leader, loyalty and tribalism can outweigh even the most damaging revelations.

Trump's defiance of political norms has permanently altered expectations for accountability. In this new paradigm, scandal is no longer a career-ending event—it can become a tool for consolidating power.

Key takeaways

- Trump's outsider brand and media savvy allowed him to dominate a disillusioned Republican base.

- His rejection of political norms and embrace of populist rhetoric redefined conservative politics.

- Loyalty to Trump became central to GOP identity, eclipsing traditional policy principles.

- Right-wing media amplified Trump's message and insulated him from political fallout, even amid scandal.

PART 02

THE RHETORIC OF MAGA- APPEAL VS. REALITY

Chapter Four
"Make America Great Again"

A Nostalgic Myth?

Perhaps the most recognizable slogan in modern American politics is "Make America Great Again" (MAGA). Simple yet powerful, it evokes nostalgia for a past era when America was perceived as more substantial, prosperous, and unified. However, what does "great" mean in this context, and for whom was America truly better? MAGA presents an idealized vision of the past, but like most nostalgic myths, it omits crucial historical context, particularly regarding economic inequality, racial injustice, and social exclusion.

The Implied Past America MAGA Longs For—Who Benefited, Who Did not?

The MAGA slogan implies that America was once in a better state and has since declined. However, pinpointing exactly when America was "great" is complicated. When asked, Trump and his supporters often refer to the post–World War II era, particularly the 1950s and early 1960s, as the ideal period (Dovere, 2016). This era is frequently portrayed as a time of economic prosperity, traditional family values, and American dominance on the world stage. However, this portrayal overlooks the many Americans excluded from that era's benefits. Trump's idealized vision of the 1950s is a profoundly selective one, ignoring the racial, gender, and class inequalities that defined the period.

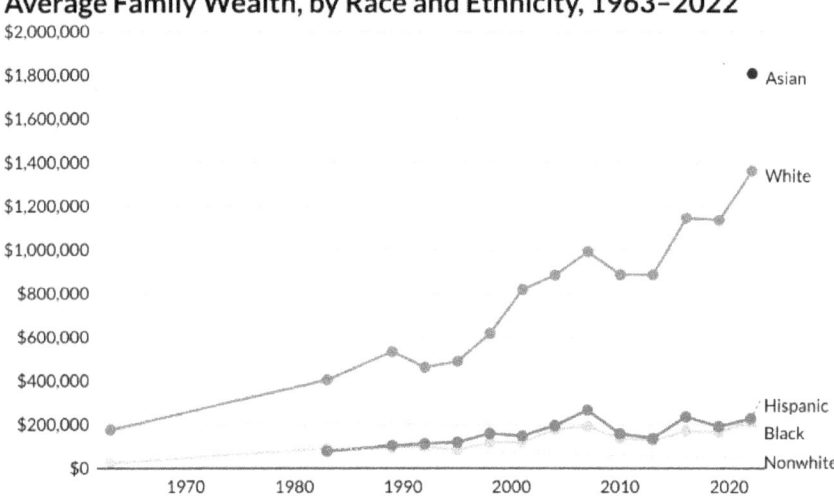

Average Family Wealth, by Race and Ethnicity, 1963–2022

Source: Urban Institute calculations from the Survey of Financial Characteristics of Consumers 1962, the Survey of Changes in Family Finances 1963, and the Survey of Consumer Finances 1983-2022.

Notes: 2022 dollars. Until 1983, the surveys categorized all people of color as "nonwhite." The Survey of Consumer Finances began disaggregating data for Black and Hispanic families starting in 1983 and for Asian families starting in 2022. We used inflation adjustment factors from *Changes in U.S. Family Finances from 2019 to 2022: Evidence from the Survey of Consumer Finances*. No comparable data are available between 1963 and 1983.

URBAN · INSTITUTE

The 1950s and 1960s were indeed a time of economic growth. The postwar boom brought rising wages, strong labor unions, and an expanding middle class, fueled partly by government programs like the GI Bill, which helped veterans access housing and education (Katznelson, 2005). However, these benefits were not distributed equally. Black Americans were systematically excluded from many of these programs due to segregationist policies at both the federal and state levels (Rothstein,

2017). Redlining, discriminatory lending practices, and segregation in education and employment meant that while white families accumulated wealth, many Black families were locked out of this prosperity (Taylor, 2019). The nostalgic image of a "great" America in the 1950s often glosses over these injustices. The experiences of Black Americans during this period are rarely acknowledged in MAGA rhetoric. That era's "greatness" reflected the privileges afforded to white Americans, especially in suburban areas. At the same time, many communities of color remained trapped in poverty and denied fundamental rights.

Women also faced significant constraints. The 1950s ideal of the nuclear family—with the man as breadwinner and the woman as homemaker—was more a product of economic and social expectations than a reflection of universal contentment. Women had limited career opportunities, were routinely paid less than men for the same work, and had little legal protection against workplace discrimination or sexual harassment (Coontz, 2011). The feminist movement of the 1960s and 1970s emerged in direct response to these restrictive roles. MAGA's nostalgic narrative frequently ignores these gendered inequalities, which ultimately gave rise to second-wave feminism and the broader fight for women's rights. The idealized past is often framed as a time of "order" and "family values," but it was also a time of stifling limitations and unfulfilled potential for many women.

For LGBTQ+ individuals, the mid-20th century was marked by pervasive discrimination, criminalization, and social rejection. During the Lavender Scare—a parallel to the Red Scare—government agencies targeted LGBTQ+ people as security risks (Johnson, 2004). Until the 1970s, being openly gay could lead to job loss, imprisonment, or forced institutionalization. The 1950s and 1960s were not an era of freedom and prosperity for all; they were a time when large population segments were actively oppressed. MAGA's vision of a "great America" conveniently erases the experiences of these marginalized groups, offering a nostalgic portrait of national unity and prosperity that never existed for everyone.

How Historical Context Complicates the Idea of a "Better Past"

The nostalgic vision promoted by MAGA selectively remembers the past, focusing on the benefits experienced by particular groups while ignoring the struggles of others. This revisionist history is a common feature of populist movements, where national identity is constructed around a mythologized past that contrasts with a supposedly declining present (Hochschild, 2016). However, a deeper examination reveals that the modern MAGA movement would likely oppose many policies and conditions contributing to the so-called "golden age" of American prosperity.

For example, Trump and his supporters often lament the decline of American manufacturing, citing the 1950s as a time when good-paying industrial jobs were abundant. While the U.S. did have a strong manufacturing base during that period, this prosperity depended on unique historical circumstances. After World War II, much of Europe and Asia were still recovering, giving the United States a significant economic advantage as the dominant global producer (Cowie, 2010). With the industrialized world in ruins, American businesses faced little international competition, allowing for rapid growth and the expansion of a thriving middle class. These conditions cannot be recreated in today's globalized economy, where countries like China, India, and members of the European Union have become major economic competitors. Hoping to return to a bygone era of unchallenged manufacturing dominance ignores the realities of modern international competition and economic interdependence.

Additionally, the policies that enabled 1950s prosperity—strong labor unions, high taxes on the wealthy, and large-scale government investment in infrastructure and education—starkly contrast with those supported by the contemporary MAGA movement. The era's robust manufacturing sector was sustained by unionized labor, yet today's Republican Party, including many MAGA supporters, strongly opposes labor unions and collective bargaining rights. Programs like the GI Bill and massive federal spending on highways, public education, and homeownership played a central role in expanding the middle class. However, modern MAGA rhetoric often resists comparable government investment in social programs and infrastructure. In the 1950s, the top marginal tax rate for the wealthiest Americans exceeded 90%, helping fund programs that enabled broad prosperity (Piketty, 2014). In contrast, the Trump administration prioritized tax cuts for corporations and the wealthy, undermining the fiscal strategies that once made postwar economic expansion possible.

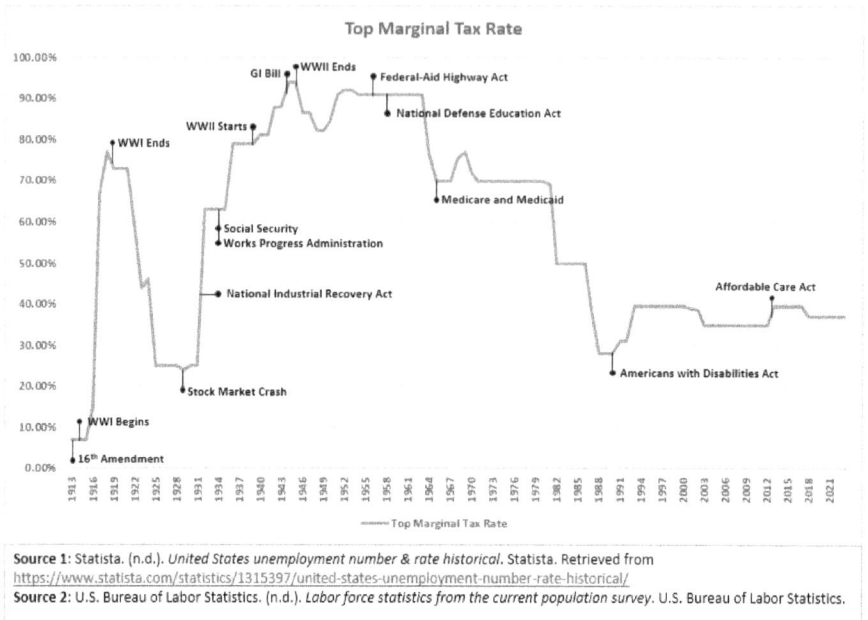

Source 1: Statista. (n.d.). *United States unemployment number & rate historical*. Statista. Retrieved from https://www.statista.com/statistics/1315397/united-states-unemployment-number-rate-historical/
Source 2: U.S. Bureau of Labor Statistics. (n.d.). *Labor force statistics from the current population survey*. U.S. Bureau of Labor Statistics.

Many MAGA supporters also express frustration over evolving cultural norms, arguing that America has become too politically correct or that traditional values have been lost (Sides, Tesler, & Vavreck, 2018). However, much of this perception stems from resistance to social progress rather than a decline in quality of life. Advances in racial and gender equality, LGBTQ+ rights, and religious diversity have significantly improved the lives of millions. However, within the MAGA worldview, these developments are often framed not as progress but as threats to a familiar social order.

Furthermore, claims that crime was lower and communities were safer in the past ignore that crime rates were much higher in the 1970s and 1980s than they are today (Federal Bureau of Investigation, 2021). Similarly, while MAGA rhetoric often suggests that America was once free of political division, history tells a different story. The 1960s and 1970s were marked by deep societal fractures, including protests against the Vietnam

War, the civil rights movement, and violent government crackdowns on dissent (Gitlin, 1987). The 1950s, too, were a time of intense political tension, primarily driven by the rise of McCarthyism and the Red Scare. Senator Joseph McCarthy's crusade against alleged communists in government and society fueled widespread fear and suspicion, dividing the nation and targeting anyone deemed a threat to American values (Parks, 1997). This political witch hunt led to the blacklisting of thousands, silenced dissent, and created a climate of fear and paranoia that permeated American life. The political tensions of the past were arguably just as severe—if not more so—than those seen today, revealing that the idea of a once-unified America is more myth than reality.

In sum, while the 1950s and 1960s were prosperous for many Americans, that prosperity was built on economic policies the modern MAGA movement would likely reject. Moreover, the global dominance that underpinned America's mid-century economic strength was primarily the result of unique historical conditions that no longer exist. Rather than longing for an era that cannot be recreated, a more pragmatic approach would involve crafting policies that confront today's economic and social challenges while acknowledging the achievements and shortcomings of the past.

The Danger of Nostalgic Nationalism

While nostalgia itself is not inherently harmful, political nostalgia, mainly when used as a foundation for policy, can be dangerous. MAGA's vision of America's past serves as a justification for reactionary policies that seek to undo decades of social progress. By romanticizing an era when women had fewer rights, racial minorities faced systemic oppression, and LGBTQ+ individuals were criminalized, the movement implicitly suggests that these conditions were acceptable or even desirable—aspects of American life. This framing ignores the social struggles and resistance movements that fought to challenge and correct these injustices. The idea of returning to an idealized past obscures the progress achieved through the civil rights movement, feminism, and LGBTQ+ advocacy—all of which worked to make America a more inclusive and equitable society. The rhetoric of "greatness" fails to account for the millions of Americans who suffered under the very systems MAGA seeks to glorify.

This form of nostalgic nationalism is not unique to the United States. Right-wing populist movements across Europe have similarly invoked idealized versions of the past, blaming immigration and globalization for perceived national decline. The Brexit campaign in the United Kingdom promoted a return to a pre–European Union, "independent" Britain. In France, Marine Le Pen's National Rally has pushed for strict immigration controls and a reassertion of French national identity. In Italy, the Lega party has capitalized on fears of cultural erosion due to immigration, framing itself as the defender of traditional Italian values. These movements often coalesce around a shared grievance, blaming external forces, such as immigrants and global trade, for their nations' supposed decline, rather than offering substantive solutions to current challenges (Norris & Inglehart, 2019).

By leaning on nostalgia, these movements create an illusion of unity and clarity, particularly during economic or social upheaval. However, this vision often overlooks the discrimination, inequality, and exclusion that characterized the so-called golden age. It also fails to address today's urgent problems, including economic inequality, environmental degradation, and rapid technological change. In this way, nostalgia becomes a political tool used to preserve power by fostering division, scapegoating globalization, and offering simplistic answers instead of grappling with the complexities of the modern world.

Trump's policies and rhetoric consistently reinforced a narrative of nostalgic nationalism. His administration's focus on immigration restrictions, opposition to critical race theory, and efforts to roll back protections for marginalized groups stemmed from the belief that America was better before these changes occurred. For example, his push for a border wall, attempts to end Deferred Action for Childhood Arrivals (DACA), and calls for a "Muslim ban" reflected a desire to return to a period when the nation was perceived as more homogenous and racially uniform. The danger of this rhetoric lies in its rejection of historical progress in favor of an imagined past that never truly existed. Rather than addressing contemporary challenges, these policies are often rooted in outdated assumptions and the fear of societal change. They aim to preserve an American identity grounded in exclusion, rather than in expanding rights and freedoms.

The idea that America was once "great" is a powerful rhetorical device—but also a profoundly misleading one. While some Americans benefited from the economic and social structures of the past, many others were actively excluded. Black Americans were denied access to post–World War II prosperity. Women were limited to narrow roles within the workforce and family. LGBTQ+ individuals faced criminalization and widespread societal rejection. The nostalgic vision promoted by MAGA overlooks these realities, romanticizing a time when many Americans were denied full citizenship and equal opportunity. That era's economic strength was also primarily fueled by the postwar weakness of other nations, a unique historical condition unlikely to be replicated. MAGA's idealized past is a selective memory—one that prioritizes the experiences of white, Christian, heterosexual men while ignoring the oppression endured by marginalized groups. By clinging to this exclusionary vision, the movement misses the opportunity to confront the persistent inequalities and injustices of the present.

Rather than longing for a return to an idealized past, the real challenge lies in addressing the contemporary issues fueling today's discontent—economic inequality, political polarization, and the impact of technological change. The rhetoric of nostalgia does not solve these problems; it offers a scapegoat. It shifts blame onto immigrants, minorities, and liberals instead of recognizing the structural flaws within the political and economic system that demand reform. A more constructive vision for America's future must acknowledge both the achievements and failures of its past, rather than distorting history to serve a political agenda. Confronting the full scope of American history—including the deep-rooted inequalities that have always existed—is essential for progress. Only by recognizing where the nation has fallen short can it move forward in a genuinely inclusive way and be true to its democratic ideals. Only then can we address the systemic challenges that continue to hold back meaningful social and economic advancement for all.

Key takeaways

- MAGA's nostalgic appeal selectively remembers the 1950s, ignoring racial, gender, and LGBTQ+ inequalities.

- Many postwar policies MAGA idolizes—like strong unions and high taxes on the wealthy—contradict current MAGA positions.

- The idea of a unified, "great" America overlooks the nation's history of political conflict and exclusion.

- Nostalgic nationalism offers a false sense of clarity while resisting necessary social and economic progress.

CHAPTER FIVE
The "Deep State" and Distrust in Institutions

A central characteristic of the MAGA movement is its deep distrust of institutions—government agencies, the mainstream media, the scientific community, and even the electoral system itself. This skepticism, often framed as a battle against the so-called "Deep State," has become a defining element of right-wing populism. However, how did this distrust develop, and how has Trump exploited it to consolidate power? By examining the long-standing tradition of skepticism toward government within American conservatism, we can better understand how Trump weaponized this sentiment for political gain. At its core, the "Deep State" narrative is not merely a paranoid conspiracy—it has been strategically deployed to delegitimize opposition, dismiss inconvenient facts, and justify anti-democratic behavior.

Understanding the roots of MAGA's anti-institutional sentiment requires looking both at the conservative tradition of government skepticism and the way Trump and his allies manipulated that sentiment to their advantage.

How Trump Weaponized Distrust in Government and the Media

The term "Deep State" gained traction during Trump's presidency, but its origins predate him. The concept emerged in authoritarian regimes, such as Turkey and Egypt, where military and intelligence officials were believed to be a shadow government resisting democratic control (O'Connor & Weatherall, 2019). In the United States, concerns about an unelected bureaucracy influencing policy had long circulated in conservative and libertarian circles. However, the idea remained a fringe until Trump elevated it to mainstream political discourse.

Trump's use of the "Deep State" allowed him to portray any opposition as part of a corrupt, hidden network working against the will of the people. Whether it involved intelligence agencies investigating Russian interference in the 2016 election, Justice Department officials prosecuting his allies, or public health experts contradicting his claims about COVID-19, Trump framed all institutional pushback as evidence of a vast conspiracy (Miller, 2020). This repeated narrative of victimhood not only reinforced his image as a fighter against the establishment but also served to discredit any policies or findings that conflicted with his agenda.

This tactic proved politically effective for several reasons. First, it allowed Trump to dismiss negative press and investigations as politically motivated attacks, strengthening his portrayal as a victim of entrenched elites. The more the media or government officials challenged him, the more it fed his narrative of being a lone outsider besieged by the "Deep State." Second, it tapped into existing conservative distrust of government, especially among voters who had long been skeptical of Washington elites. This distrust had deep roots in the backlash against the civil rights movement, the fallout from Watergate, and more recent frustrations over trade, immigration, and economic inequality. Third, the "Deep State" narrative provided a flexible framework that could explain away almost any outcome. If Trump's policies failed, it was due to sabotage. If he lost an election, it was because of institutional corruption.

This narrative became so deeply embedded that many of his supporters remained loyal even after Trump's claims were thoroughly debunked. The refusal to accept verified facts—whether regarding the 2020 election results or the severity of the COVID-19 pandemic—became part of a broader rejection of expert knowledge and institutional authority. Trump's "alternative facts" approach to governance reinforced this rejection, fostering an environment in which objective truth was treated with suspicion and political dissent was framed as evidence of a conspiracy.

The Role of Right-Wing Media in Eroding Trust

MAGA's institutional distrust has been amplified by a right-wing media ecosystem that thrives on fueling skepticism and outrage. Fox News, talk radio, and conservative online outlets have spent decades portraying the mainstream media as hopelessly biased, creating an alternate media reality for millions of Americans. This ecosystem has consistently cast itself as the defender of "true" American values, positioning liberal media outlets as enemies of the people. Trump's presidency accelerated this trend, as networks like One America News Network (OANN) and Newsmax positioned themselves as even more extreme alternatives, openly embracing conspiracy theories (Benkler, Faris, & Roberts, 2018). These outlets not only catered to Trump's base but actively encouraged a parallel reality—one in which truth is malleable and any information that contradicts the MAGA narrative is dismissed as "fake news."

One of the most significant ways right-wing media has eroded trust in institutions is through relentless attacks on the mainstream press. Trump popularized the term "fake news" to discredit any reporting that challenged his narrative, and his supporters quickly adopted the phrase to dismiss inconvenient facts (Waisbord, 2018). This was more than a critique of media bias— it was a calculated effort to undermine the idea that objective reporting and verifiable facts have value in public discourse. By labeling unfavorable coverage as fake, Trump turned the media into an "enemy of the people," a tactic with far-reaching consequences. It fostered an environment where criticism was no longer seen as legitimate oversight but as part of a coordinated, partisan attack. The result is a fragmented information landscape, where public trust in journalism has eroded and political narratives are shaped more by ideological loyalty than factual accuracy.

Figure 1
Level of Confidence in Science by Political Party, 1974 – 2022

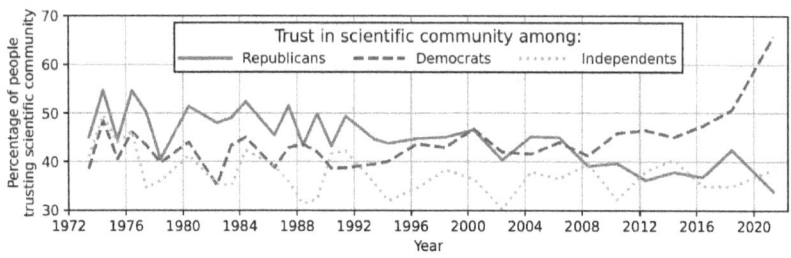

Source: The General Social Survey, the latest conducted from December 1, 2020 – May 3, 2021. Auditors asked, "I am going to name some institutions in this country. As far as the people running these institutions are concerned, would you say you have a great deal of confidence, only some confidence, or hardly any confidence at all in them?" Figure by Alexander Kaurov.

This rhetoric of distrust extended beyond politics and the media—it reached into science and public health, with devastating consequences.

The COVID-19 pandemic exposed the power of right-wing media to shape public perception and erode trust in scientific institutions. Public health authorities such as the Centers for Disease Control and Prevention (CDC) and the World Health Organization (WHO) became frequent targets of conservative skepticism. From the outset, right-wing media fueled conspiracy theories about the virus's origins, the effectiveness of lockdowns, and the safety of vaccines (Lewandowsky, 2021). Trump himself amplified this misinformation, downplaying the severity of the virus, undermining mask-wearing, and promoting unproven treatments—all of which were echoed across conservative media outlets.

Despite overwhelming scientific evidence, millions of Americans rejected basic health guidelines because they had been conditioned to distrust experts. This rejection of science was not merely a response to a public health crisis—it was part of a broader narrative that framed elite institutions, including academia and the scientific community, as untrustworthy and self-serving. By reinforcing the belief that public health experts were either incompetent or corrupt, right-wing media allowed dangerous misinformation to flourish, directly contributing to a higher death toll and prolonging the pandemic.

This pattern of distrust has extended to the electoral system as well. Following the 2020 election, Trump and his allies propagated baseless claims of widespread voter fraud, despite the absence of credible evidence supporting these allegations (Rosenfeld, 2021). Conservative media outlets amplified these assertions, with platforms like Fox News, Newsmax, and One America News repeatedly featuring guests who questioned the election's legitimacy. This reinforcement of misinformation created a feedback loop in which Trump's claims gained traction among his supporters, deepening skepticism about the electoral process.

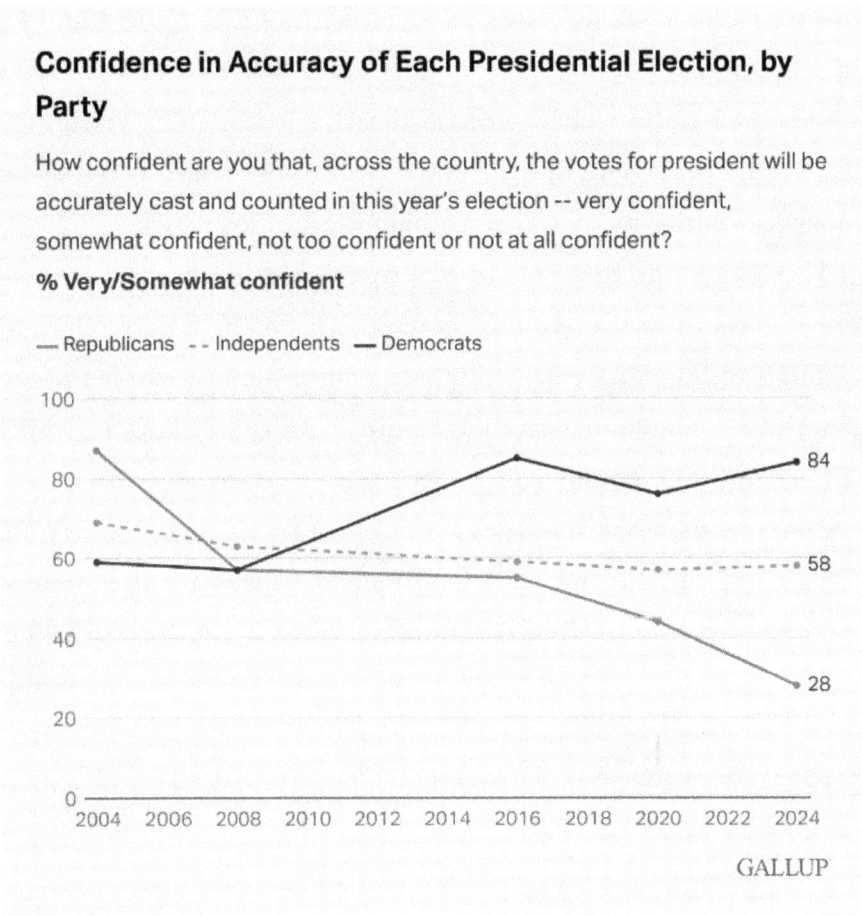

As a result, trust in American democracy declined significantly within the Republican electorate. A CNN poll found that approximately 66% of Republicans viewed President Joe Biden's 2020 election win as illegitimate (Enten, 2023). This distrust is historically unprecedented in modern U.S. politics and marks a significant shift in how large population segments perceive election integrity. The consequences of this erosion of faith culminated in the January 6th insurrection, when thousands of Trump supporters stormed the Capitol in an attempt to prevent the certification of Biden's victory. While the attack was widely condemned, the belief that the election was stolen has persisted, contributing to the continued radicalization of a segment of the Republican base. The assault on the Capitol was not merely a physical breach—it was an attack on the democratic process itself, fueled by a media ecosystem that had spent months distorting reality and undermining institutional trust.

The long-term effects of this distrust extend far beyond January 6th. Efforts to restrict voting access, based on the false premise of widespread fraud, have gained momentum in Republican-led states. Since 2020, numerous state legislatures have passed laws imposing stricter voter ID requirements, reducing access to mail-in voting, and granting partisan officials greater control over election administration (Brennan Center for Justice, 2023). While these laws are often framed as election security reforms, they disproportionately affect marginalized communities, including racial minorities, low-income voters, and people with disabilities. By weaponizing election distrust, Republican leaders have advanced policies that entrench political power rather than address legitimate electoral concerns.

Moreover, election denialism has shaped not only policy but also candidate selection within the Republican Party. Many GOP candidates in the 2022 and 2024 elections ran on election fraud narratives, with some refusing to commit to accepting results unless they won. This signals a growing willingness among conservative politicians to undermine democratic norms for short-term political advantage. Even after their losses, candidates like Kari Lake in Arizona and Doug Mastriano in Pennsylvania continued to push baseless claims of fraud, reinforcing the notion that elections are only legitimate when Republicans win.

At its core, this manufactured distrust in elections serves a broader political strategy: by convincing their base that the system is rigged, right-wing leaders justify extreme measures—voter suppression laws, partisan gerrymandering, and attempts to subvert future election outcomes. This poses an existential threat to democracy, which depends on the consent of the governed and the peaceful transfer of power. Without trust in the electoral system, democratic legitimacy erodes, fueling polarization and the risk of political violence.

Polling indicates that this distrust has had lasting effects, with partisan divisions over election integrity widening in the years since the insurrection. Without a concerted effort to restore confidence in democratic institutions—through transparency, civic education, and media accountability—the United States risks continued democratic backsliding, where election skepticism becomes a permanent feature of conservative politics rather than a temporary reaction to Trump's presidency.

The Erosion of Faith in Democracy and Expert Knowledge

One of the most dangerous consequences of MAGA's institutional distrust is its impact on democracy. When large segments of the population no longer trust the electoral process, the judicial system, or the media, the foundations of democracy become unstable. Trump's insistence that the 2020 election was rigged was not simply an attack on Joe Biden—it was an attack on the legitimacy of American democracy. His repeated claims that the election was "stolen," despite overwhelming evidence to the contrary, created a narrative that cast doubt on the very foundation of the democratic process. This represents a direct assault on the core principle of democratic governance: the peaceful transfer of power essential to political stability.

The erosion of trust in electoral processes is not limited to Trump's supporters; it reflects a broader trend in which political narratives are increasingly shaped by emotion and loyalty rather than factual evidence. Public opinion data underscores this shift. A 2021 poll found that 58% of Republicans believed the 2020 election was stolen, despite no credible evidence supporting the claim (Ipsos, 2021). Similarly, trust in government agencies has plummeted among conservatives, with institutions like the FBI and the Department of Justice increasingly viewed as politically compromised. When a significant portion of the electorate believes that the electoral system is fundamentally corrupt, the nation faces a critical threat to its democratic integrity.

This rejection of institutional legitimacy extends beyond elections—it has also severely undermined public trust in expert knowledge. Climate change denial, vaccine skepticism, and distrust in academia have all been fueled by the same anti-institutional mindset promoted by the MAGA movement (Gauchat, 2012). The refusal to accept scientifically supported facts in favor of ideological beliefs has led to policy paralysis, especially on urgent issues like climate change, where large segments of the public routinely dismiss broad scientific consensus. The COVID-19 pandemic further exposed this divide, as public health authorities such as the CDC and WHO faced fierce backlash from political figures and media outlets that cast them as symbols of a corrupt establishment. As a result, expert guidance on health and safety was disregarded, contributing directly to the pandemic's mismanagement and prolonging its impact.

Moreover, the rejection of facts and expertise has given way to the acceptance of fringe conspiracy theories. In addition to denying the 2020 election results, some population segments have embraced ideas like Flat Earth theory. While often dismissed as absurd, the popularity of such beliefs reveals a deeper issue: a growing willingness to reject expert consensus in favor of disinformation. This trend is not limited to a few extremists—it reflects a broader cultural shift in which people increasingly choose alternative narratives that align with their political or ideological preferences, even when they contradict overwhelming evidence. Fueled by the MAGA movement and right-wing media, this shift contributes to a more significant erosion of truth itself, where facts are treated as flexible and political loyalty takes precedence over rational debate.

A particularly troubling manifestation of this trend is the right-wing tendency to ridicule scientific studies that challenge their worldview. Conservative media and politicians frequently dismiss research as "silly" or "wasteful," mainly when it explores topics they consider trivial or politically inconvenient. Studies addressing climate change, racial disparities, gender identity, or the psychological effects of misinformation are often mocked rather than seriously engaged. A common tactic is highlighting government-funded research that, taken out of context, appears frivolous, ignoring its broader scientific relevance. For example, research on the sexual behavior of animals has been derided as "liberal waste," despite its contributions to evolutionary biology and genetics (Gross, 2016).

One of the most infamous examples of this strategy is the so-called "shrimp on a treadmill" study, which Republican politicians and right-wing media frequently cited as evidence of wasteful government spending. The study, which examined the effects of environmental stressors on shrimp mobility, was part of legitimate research into marine biology and ecological health. However, it was repeatedly taken out of context and mocked to discredit federally funded scientific research (Zimmer, 2011). This misrepresentation is a deliberate tactic aimed at fostering skepticism toward scientific institutions and dismissing research that does not align with conservative ideology.

This approach is part of a broader effort to delegitimize entire fields of study, particularly the social sciences and climate science. By portraying academia as inherently biased and out of touch with "real American" concerns, MAGA rhetoric encourages distrust of expert knowledge while promoting alternative narratives often grounded in misinformation. The consequences of this strategy are far-reaching: it discourages evidence-based policymaking and promotes a culture in which personal opinion is treated as equal to peer-reviewed research. When scientific findings are routinely dismissed as "woke" or "agenda-driven," the ability to address pressing societal challenges—from public health crises to environmental degradation—is severely undermined.

The MAGA movement's distrust in institutions is not merely a spontaneous reaction—it is the culmination of decades of conservative skepticism toward government, intensified by Trump's rhetoric and amplified by right-wing media. The "Deep State" narrative has become a powerful political tool, enabling Trump and his allies to discredit opposition, justify extreme actions, and delegitimize democratic institutions. By casting government agencies, media organizations, and experts as part of a conspiracy to sabotage American greatness, Trump cultivated an environment in which objective reality is constantly questioned. This narrative allowed him to reject any facts contradicting his views, further deepening the divide between his supporters and the broader public.

The consequences of this institutional distrust extend beyond Trump himself. The erosion of faith in government, media, and expert knowledge poses a serious threat to the stability of American democracy and civil society. When millions reject basic facts and view all institutions as inherently corrupt, rational political discourse becomes nearly impossible, and effective governance breaks down. Democracy depends on a shared commitment to truth—without it, the capacity for collective action diminishes, and political polarization intensifies. As the MAGA movement has shown, once skepticism toward key institutions becomes deeply embedded, it can have long-lasting, destabilizing effects. Constructive dialogue becomes almost impossible when large portions of the population are invested in alternative realities.

The rise of conspiracy theories—from election fraud to Flat Earth—reflects this broader cultural shift toward rejecting expertise and institutional authority. It signals the growing danger of a society where belief becomes untethered from fact and loyalty to political ideology takes precedence over a commitment to shared truths. The long-term challenge will be rebuilding trust in institutions and, in doing so, protecting the future of American democracy.

Key takeaways

- MAGA exploits long-standing conservative skepticism of institutions to undermine trust in democracy and expertise.

- The "Deep State" narrative frames opposition as a conspiracy, justifying authoritarian behavior.

- Right-wing media plays a major role in spreading misinformation and eroding faith in science, media, and elections.

- This distrust fuels election denialism, public health crises, and a fragmented, polarized society.

CHAPTER SIX

The "America First" Illusion

The MAGA movement's commitment to "America First" reflects a shift toward a nationalist framework prioritizing American interests in trade, immigration, and foreign policy. While the slogan resonates with many who feel global institutions and foreign competitors have exploited the United States, the reality of "America First" policies is far more complex. This framework offers a simplistic view of America's role in the world and the realities of global interdependence. It reduces nuanced international dynamics to a binary "us vs. them" mentality, obscuring the intricacies of trade, diplomacy, and cooperation.

Rather than restoring American dominance, MAGA's economic isolationism and immigration restrictions have often produced unintended consequences, frequently harming the very workers and industries they were intended to protect. The refusal to acknowledge the interconnectedness of global markets has fueled a false narrative: that "closing off" America will lead to economic resurgence. In reality, such isolationist policies disrupt supply chains, raise consumer prices, and destabilize industries that depend on global trade. This chapter explores how Trump's rhetoric on trade and immigration oversimplifies economic realities, creating the illusion of strength while undermining long-term prosperity.

The Myth of Economic Nationalism: Trade Wars and Their Consequences

One of Trump's signature "America First" policies was his aggressive approach to trade. He frequently blamed past administrations for negotiating "bad deals" that allowed other countries, especially China, to exploit the United States. His proposed solution was a series of import tariffs, which he claimed would restore American manufacturing and reduce the trade deficit. Trump's populist promise to return manufacturing jobs by targeting imports appealed to working-class Americans, particularly in communities struck by outsourcing.

However, the impact of Trump's trade policies was far more damaging than his rhetoric suggested. The trade war with China escalated into tariffs on hundreds of billions of dollars in goods, triggering retaliatory tariffs that hurt American farmers and manufacturers. A study by Amiti, Redding, and Weinstein (2019) found that the cost of these tariffs was primarily borne by American consumers and businesses, not foreign exporters. This led to higher prices for goods and reduced global competitiveness for U.S. companies, especially those reliant on inexpensive imports to keep costs down.

The agricultural sector was particularly hard hit. Once a major buyer of American soybeans, China responded with tariffs on U.S. agricultural goods. As a result, American farmers suffered significant losses, prompting the Trump administration to issue billions in bailout payments to offset the damage (Bown, 2020). This reliance on subsidies highlighted the fragility of the "America First" economic approach, which offered short-term relief rather than addressing long-standing structural challenges. Instead of revitalizing American industry, the trade war exposed the dangers of assuming economic isolation would lead to prosperity.

Trump also withdrew from the Trans-Pacific Partnership (TPP), a multilateral trade agreement many economists argued would have strengthened U.S. influence in the Asia-Pacific region (Petri & Plummer, 2016). In comparison, Trump framed the TPP as a "globalist" scheme that hurt American workers, exiting the agreement weakened America's ability to shape trade rules in the region, and opened the door for China to expand its economic influence. In effect, Trump's "America First" policy isolated the U.S. while simultaneously ceding global leadership to its chief rival.

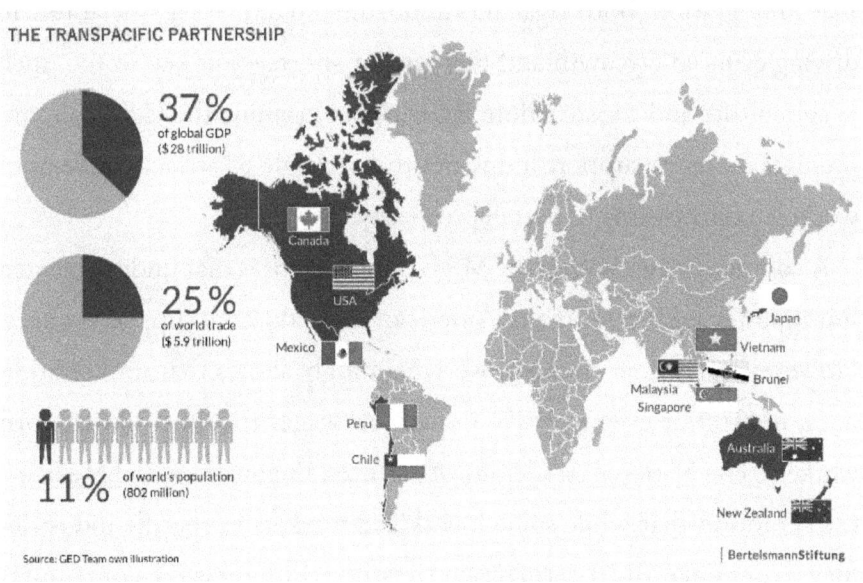

Far from achieving economic independence, the "America First" trade agenda disrupted supply chains, increased consumer costs, and failed to deliver on promises to bring back manufacturing jobs. The trade wars revealed how economic isolationism creates a false sense of security, ignoring the interconnected global economy that requires collaboration rather than unilateral action. Moreover, MAGA's policies lacked a coherent, long-term plan to rebuild American industry without compounding existing challenges such as automation, labor shortages, and the decline of skilled manufacturing jobs.

The Reality of Immigration and the U.S. Economy

Trump's hardline stance on immigration—framing it as a threat to American jobs, public safety, and national identity—is central to the "America First" philosophy. While this rhetoric resonates with some, it oversimplifies complex economic realities. Numerous studies have shown that immigration, both legal and undocumented, plays a crucial role in driving economic growth and filling labor shortages in key sectors such as agriculture and construction. Rather than harming the U.S. economy, immigrants often support industries that struggle to attract native-born workers, contributing to overall prosperity.

A common claim within the MAGA movement is that undocumented immigrants take jobs from American citizens and suppress wages. However, economic research overwhelmingly shows that immigration has a neutral or even positive impact on wages for most native-born workers. The National Academies of Sciences, Engineering, and Medicine (2017) found that while some low-skilled workers in specific industries may experience short-term wage pressure, immigration contributes substantially to economic growth and innovation.

Moreover, immigrants—both documented and undocumented—play vital roles in labor-intensive sectors like agriculture, construction, and caregiving. These industries are critical to the U.S. economy, yet often suffer from labor shortages when immigrant workers are excluded. This dynamic became especially clear under Trump's immigration policies. In 2019, for example, ICE raids on poultry processing plants in Mississippi led to the deportation of hundreds of undocumented workers. The jobs left behind went largely unfilled by native-born workers, resulting in production slowdowns (Jordan, 2019). This illustrates a key point: reducing immigration does not automatically create job opportunities for Americans—it can instead lead to labor gaps, higher consumer prices, and decreased productivity.

Another often-overlooked aspect of immigration is immigrants' contribution to the U.S. tax system. Both documented and undocumented immigrants make significant tax contributions, including substantial payments into Social Security. In 2022, undocumented immigrants paid approximately $25.7 billion in Social Security taxes, despite being ineligible to receive benefits due to their immigration status. These contributions are vital to the sustainability of Social Security, primarily as the program relies on a growing workforce to support an aging population. The influx of younger immigrants helps offset demographic shifts, strengthening the system's long-term financial health.

In addition, immigrants contribute to other essential public services through various taxes, including sales, excise, and property taxes. In 2022 alone, undocumented immigrants paid $96.7 billion in federal, state, and local taxes, including $37.3 billion directed to state and local governments. These funds support infrastructure, education, healthcare, and other public services that benefit the entire population. Immigrants play a critical role in sustaining and enhancing the quality of life across the United States by participating in the tax system.

In this light, immigrants are not a burden on the U.S. economy but a net benefit. They support the Social Security system, help fill crucial labor shortages, and substantially contribute to public revenue. The claim that immigrants take more than they give is not supported by economic evidence and ignores their broader contributions to the nation's fiscal and social well-being.

The Crime and Public Safety Myth

Another key claim within the "America First" narrative is that immigrants—especially undocumented ones—pose a significant threat to public safety. Trump frequently cited anecdotal cases of crimes committed by undocumented immigrants as justification for policies such as building a border wall and expanding ICE enforcement.

However, empirical evidence consistently contradicts this narrative. Studies show that immigrants, including undocumented individuals, commit crimes at lower rates than native-born Americans. Light and Miller (2018) found that immigrants generally commit fewer violent crimes, challenging the stereotype of the "dangerous immigrant." Similarly, Ousey and Kubrin (2018) found that higher immigration levels are associated with lower crime rates in communities. Immigrants often strengthen neighborhoods by contributing to social networks that promote safety and cohesion, directly undermining the claim that they threaten public security.

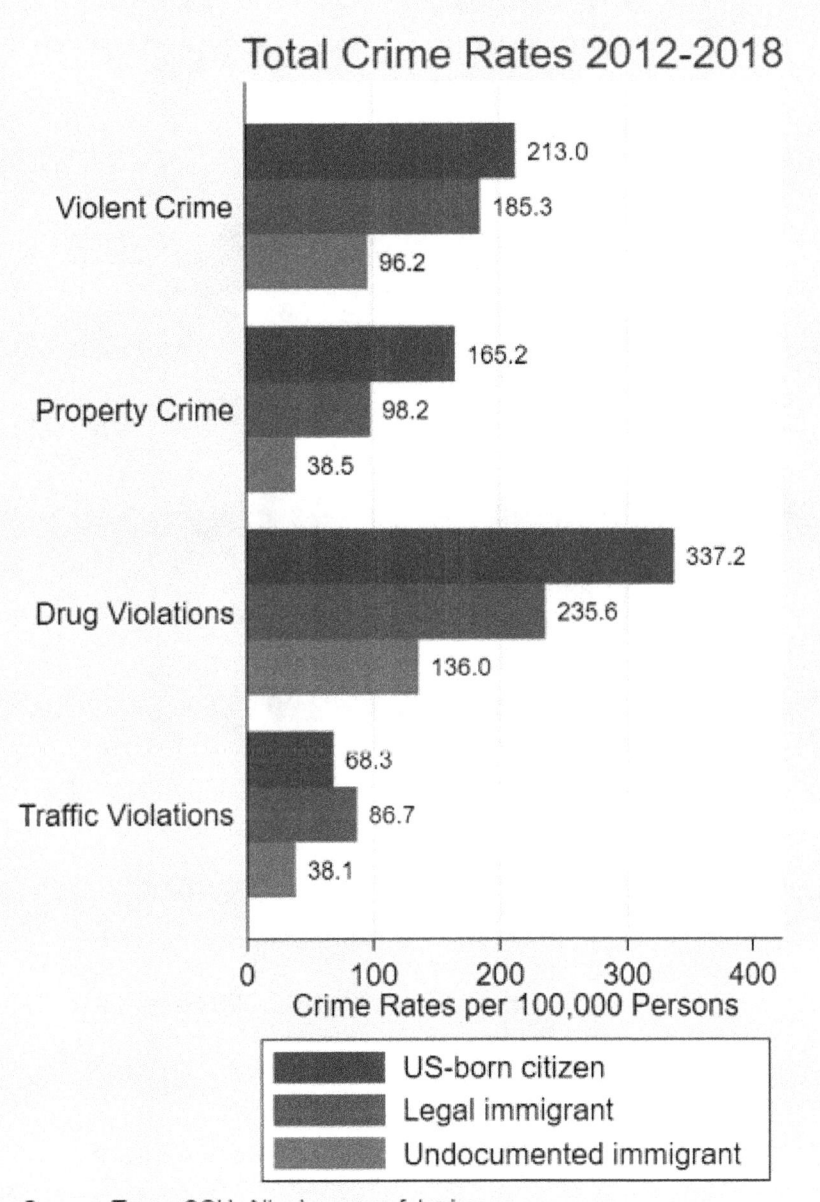

Source: Texas CCH. All crimes are felonies.
Legal immigrants include naturalized citizens.

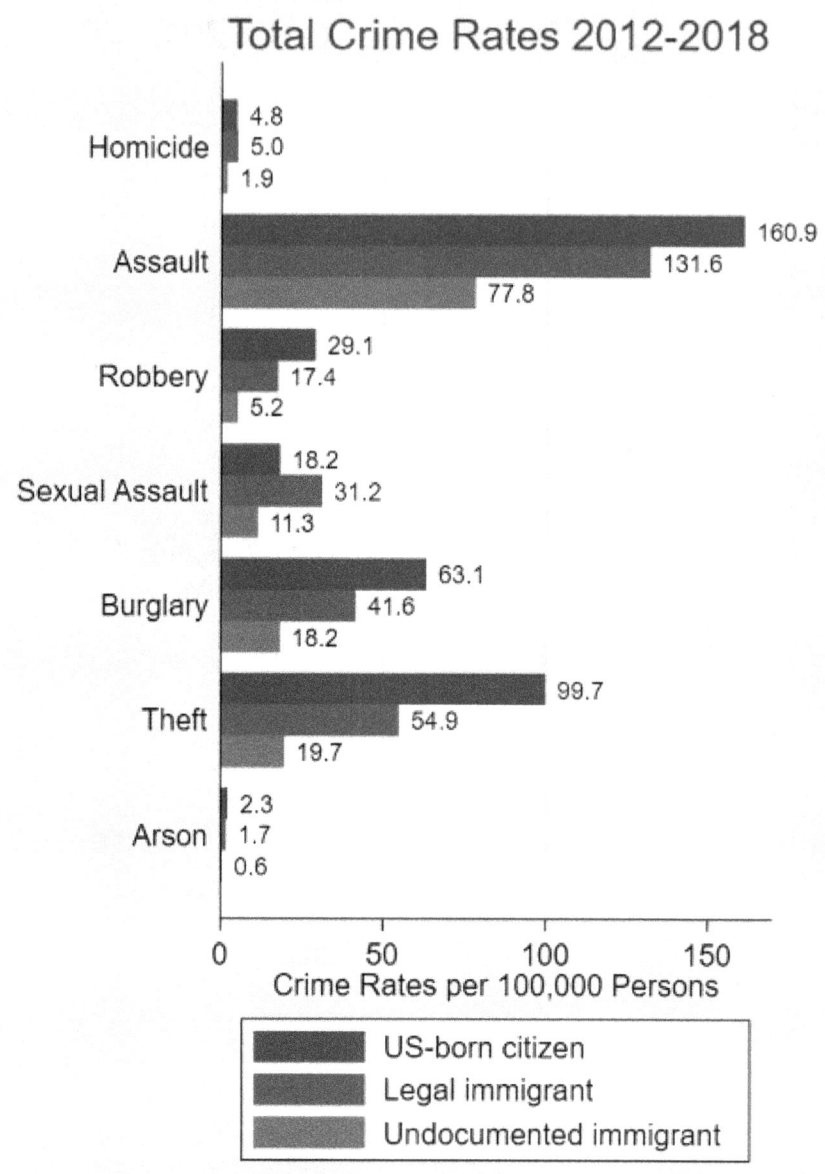

This evidence suggests that the myth of the immigrant-as-criminal is mainly political rhetoric. Rather than engaging with facts, the MAGA movement has strategically weaponized the fear of immigration to rally support and justify divisive policies. These policies do not align with the actual needs of communities and often divert attention from the more significant factors contributing to crime, such as economic inequality, systemic racism, and inadequate access to education and mental health services.

Moreover, framing immigrants as criminals has serious social consequences. It fosters discrimination, erodes trust between immigrant communities and law enforcement, and exacerbates racial and ethnic tensions. Immigrants unfairly labeled as dangerous face increased scrutiny and hostility, making it more difficult for them to participate in society and contribute to the economy fully. This divisive rhetoric harms not only immigrant communities but also the broader social fabric, weakening the cohesion that is essential for building safe and inclusive neighborhoods.

Ultimately, the persistent myth of immigrant criminality serves to distract from the structural causes of crime. Instead of scapegoating immigrants, policymakers should focus on addressing poverty, unemployment, unequal access to education, and other root causes of crime. By continuing to frame immigration as a public safety threat, the MAGA movement avoids confronting the complex economic and social challenges that demand genuine, evidence-based solutions.

Family Separations and the Human Cost of "America First"

Perhaps the most infamous immigration policy under the Trump administration was the "zero tolerance" approach, which led to the separation of thousands of migrant families at the U.S. border. Under this policy, children were taken from their parents and placed in detention facilities, often with no transparent process for reunification (Habbach, Hampton, & Mishori, 2020). The policy was intended to deter illegal immigration by imposing severe consequences for crossing the border. Instead, it became one of the most widely condemned aspects of Trump's immigration agenda, criticized for both its cruelty and its administrative chaos.

While Trump defended the policy as a necessary deterrent, its implementation lacked the basic infrastructure to track and reunite separated families. The trauma experienced by the children, many of whom were placed in overcrowded, unsanitary conditions, was worsened by the absence of a clear reunification plan. Reports later revealed that many parents were deported without their children, and in numerous cases, the government had no means of identifying or locating the children after the separation (Dickerson, 2021). The immense psychological and emotional toll on these families is immeasurable. However, it underscores a deeper issue: the "America First" rhetoric failed to offer a solution that was either compassionate or effective.

This policy exposed the moral contradictions inherent in the "America First" approach. While Trump's rhetoric framed family separation as a necessary enforcement tool to protect national security and uphold American values, the actual outcomes starkly contradicted those ideals. Rather than demonstrating strength, the policy revealed a lack of basic humanity in governance, treating children as collateral damage in a political strategy. It was widely condemned as a violation of human rights and an affront to the long-standing American value of family unity. Instead of fostering a society grounded in compassion and fairness, the policy served to divide, stigmatize, and dehumanize those seeking a better life in the United States.

The False Promise of Economic Isolationism

The core flaw of the "America First" agenda lies in its failure to recognize the interconnected nature of the modern global economy. Trump's policies—particularly on trade and immigration—sought to isolate the U.S. from critical global economic forces such as supply chains, labor markets, and international trade agreements. The goal was to bring back jobs and restore national strength. However, this approach ignored the reality that the U.S. economy, like all advanced economies, is deeply integrated with global markets. Isolating the country through tariffs, restrictive immigration policies, and withdrawal from international agreements introduced inefficiencies and raised costs for American consumers and businesses. These measures did not deliver the promised benefits of economic independence. Instead, they disrupted established supply chains, inflated prices, and stifled growth.

For example, Trump's tariffs were promoted to revive U.S. manufacturing and penalize foreign competitors, especially China. In practice, however, the tariffs created trade disruptions that harmed American businesses more than they helped. They increased the cost of goods, reduced U.S. competitiveness abroad, and damaged industries dependent on imports. Similarly, Trump's immigration crackdowns, framed as efforts to protect American jobs, led to labor shortages in essential industries such as agriculture, construction, and hospitality. These sectors struggled to find enough workers, resulting in decreased productivity and higher operating costs. Far from supporting American workers, these policies destabilized labor markets and weakened the industries they aimed to protect.

Despite these failures, the "America First" narrative remains a potent political tool. It provides a simple, emotionally resonant explanation for complex economic and social challenges by blaming "outsiders"—whether immigrants, foreign workers, or international competitors. This scapegoating deflects attention from systemic problems within the U.S. economy, such as corporate consolidation, wage stagnation, and weakened labor protections. Rather than pursuing meaningful structural reforms, the nationalist rhetoric favors blame over solutions. Real progress requires investments in worker protections, expanded access to education, and support for technological innovation, not policies rooted in fear and exclusion.

True economic prosperity in the 21st century cannot be achieved through isolation. It demands engagement, cooperation, and policies built on collaboration with global partners. The false promise of "America First" may yield short-term political gains, but it comes at the cost of long-term economic and diplomatic strength. To succeed in a globalized world, the U.S. must move beyond protectionist ideologies and embrace strategies that are inclusive, evidence-based, and focused on addressing the root causes of inequality, while reinforcing its leadership in the international community.

Key takeaways

- Economic nationalism under Trump led to trade wars that hurt American consumers and farmers more than foreign rivals.

- Immigration policies disrupted industries reliant on immigrant labor without solving job shortages.

- "America First" rhetoric ignored global interdependence and often weakened U.S. influence abroad.

- The slogan oversimplifies complex economic issues and promotes isolation over long-term solutions.

CHAPTER SEVEN
The Culture War as a Political Strategy

Through its focus on social values, identity, and national belonging, the MAGA movement has skillfully weaponized the "culture war"—the ongoing political and ideological struggle over morality, social issues, and American identity—to rally and energize its base. While traditional conservatism once emphasized economic issues such as tax cuts and deregulation, Trump-era populism has shifted the focus to cultural grievances. Central to this strategy is the attack on "wokeism," a term often used pejoratively by conservatives to describe progressive movements advocating for racial, gender, and LGBTQ+ equality. The demonization of LGBTQ+ rights, criticism of public education, and hostility toward the media have all become defining features of MAGA's messaging. These emotionally charged issues have allowed the movement to engage its base and sustain momentum, even without significant economic policy achievements. By framing cultural and social changes as existential threats to American identity, MAGA has transformed everyday issues, such as education, race, and gender equality, into political battlegrounds, ensuring its supporters remain mobilized and committed.

The Role of Grievance Politics in Uniting MAGA's Base

At the heart of MAGA's culture war is the belief that traditional American values are under siege. Trump and his allies have framed issues ranging from immigration to gender identity as direct threats to the nation's core principles. This powerful narrative centers on abstract, emotional concerns rather than measurable policy outcomes. In a political environment where concrete promises often go unfulfilled, MAGA's cultural grievances remain adaptable, allowing the movement to continually reshape its message in response to shifting societal trends. This strategy has helped maintain a sense of urgency and victimhood among its base, reinforcing that they are locked in a battle to preserve their way of life.

This appeal to a perceived threatened majority echoes Richard Nixon's "silent majority" strategy from the late 1960s, which positioned him as a defender of ordinary Americans, mainly white, middle-class voters, against the perceived chaos of social movements, urban unrest, and cultural liberalism. Just as Nixon portrayed his supporters as besieged by radical change, MAGA uses similar rhetoric to present its base as the last defenders of American values. However, while Nixon's message centered on law and order in response to civil rights protests and anti-war activism, Trump expanded the battlefield to include immigration, gender identity, and political correctness.

A central component of this narrative is the idea that "real" Americans—often implicitly defined as white, Christian, rural, and conservative—are being displaced by progressive elites, people of color, and LGBTQ+ individuals. This "us vs. them" framing unites a broad coalition, from working-class white voters to suburban conservatives, under the banner of protecting traditional values. It provides convenient scapegoats—liberal elites, immigrants, and social justice movements—who are blamed for undermining the nation's cultural and social fabric. This narrative fosters a strong sense of collective identity among MAGA supporters, allowing them to feel justified in their political views and empowered by their participation in a more significant cultural movement, even if their material conditions remain unchanged.

This tactic also draws heavily from the Republican Party's "Southern Strategy," which emerged in the late 1960s to realign the party's base by appealing to white Southern voters who felt alienated by the civil rights movement and racial integration. By emphasizing issues such as states' rights, crime, and opposition to affirmative action, the Southern Strategy exploited racial anxieties without explicitly invoking race—a technique known as dog-whistle politics. Trump's messaging operates similarly. Phrases like "Make America Great Again" implicitly appeal to voters who feel that the nation's increasing diversity has come at their expense. His repeated attacks on critical race theory, diversity initiatives, and "woke" culture serve the same function as past Republican efforts to portray racial progress as a threat to traditional American values. By blending the cultural victimhood of Nixon's "silent majority" with the racial undertones of the Southern Strategy, Trump has reenergized and expanded a political coalition that continues to define the modern GOP through the MAGA movement.

The appeal of MAGA's cultural messaging goes beyond political strategy. Research has shown that cultural resentment, rather than economic anxiety, was the strongest predictor of support for Trump in 2016. According to Sides, Tesler, and Vavreck (2018), voters who believed white Americans were losing their dominant status in society were significantly more likely to support Trump, even after accounting for income and education levels. This suggests that the MAGA movement is driven not only by economic frustration but also by a more profound resistance to social change, particularly about race, gender, and the country's growing diversity. Within this framework, economic concerns are often seen as symptoms of cultural decline: issues like job loss or wage stagnation are not merely economic problems, but consequences of a perceived departure from traditional American values.

MAGA's success lies in its ability to channel these cultural anxieties into a compelling political narrative—one that frames societal change as a threat to national identity. The movement translates these fears into political action by offering emotionally resonant, oversimplified solutions: build a wall, ban critical race theory, oppose the "radical left." These gestures promise a return to an idealized version of America. However, this focus on cultural issues often distracts from the more complex and structural causes of economic inequality and social fragmentation, such as stagnant wages, declining labor protections, and corporate practices prioritizing profit over worker well-being. In this way, the culture war functions as a smokescreen, allowing MAGA to mobilize its base by emphasizing identity and grievance rather than addressing the systemic issues that truly drive economic and social discontent.

Misinformation and the Manufactured Panic Over "Wokeism"

The MAGA movement's culture war is primarily driven by a manufactured panic over "wokeism," a term that has been stripped of its original meaning and repurposed as a catch-all label for progressive social change. Initially coined by Black activists to describe awareness of racial injustice, "woke" has been appropriated by right-wing politicians and media to signify an oppressive left-wing ideology. This shift has turned the term into a political weapon, framing a vague "woke agenda" as a threat to traditional American values. In reality, this narrative is more about sowing division than describing any coherent movement.

Misinformation about Critical Race Theory (CRT) has been central to the panic over "wokeism." CRT, an academic framework developed in the 1970s and primarily studied in law schools, explores how systemic racism is embedded in legal systems and public policy, rather than existing solely as individual prejudice (Delgado & Stefancic, 2017). Conservative activists, notably Christopher Rufo, have deliberately distorted CRT's meaning to make it politically toxic. "The goal is to have the public read something crazy in the newspaper and immediately think 'critical race theory,'" Rufo tweeted in 2021. "We have decodified the term and will recodify it to annex the entire range of cultural constructions unpopular with Americans." This strategy has enabled right-wing media and politicians to falsely portray CRT as an attempt to shame white Americans or indoctrinate children in schools. The resulting moral panic has fueled book bans, teacher censorship, and restrictive education policies in Republican-led states, not to combat CRT itself, which was never part of K–12 curricula, but to suppress broader conversations about racism and inequality.

Similarly, MAGA figures have exploited fears around LGBTQ+ inclusion, mainly by pushing the baseless claim that LGBTQ+ educators and allies are "grooming" children. Despite a complete lack of evidence, this allegation has gained traction in conservative circles (Ferguson, 2022). Laws like Florida's "Don't Say Gay" bill, which restricts classroom discussions of gender and sexuality, are part of a broader campaign to roll back LGBTQ+ rights under the pretense of protecting children from inappropriate content. These culture war flashpoints are not merely ideological conflicts; they are calculated political tools intended to energize conservative voters by tapping into emotional fears, especially those involving children.

Research shows that moral panics, particularly those centered on protecting children, are highly effective at mobilizing political engagement (Jenkins, 2021). By framing progressive policies as existential threats, MAGA leaders can galvanize their base and maintain loyalty, even when economic promises go unfulfilled. In this way, the "wokeism" narrative functions as both a distraction from systemic issues, such as economic inequality, and a unifying force that keeps conservative supporters focused on divisive social battles rather than broader structural concerns.

The "War on Religion" and Christian Nationalism

Christian nationalism has become a powerful force within the MAGA movement, promoting the belief that Christianity is under attack despite its continued dominance in American society. MAGA figures frequently claim that religious Americans face persecution, using concerns about secularization, LGBTQ+ rights, and reproductive freedom to stoke cultural grievances. This manufactured sense of crisis fosters a narrative of victimhood among conservative Christians, allowing MAGA leaders to cast themselves as defenders of faith while advancing policies that impose religious ideology on broader society.

More than four-in-ten Americans think the U.S. should be a 'Christian nation'

% who say ...

	The founders of America <u>originally intended</u> for the U.S. to be a "Christian nation"		The U.S. <u>is now</u> a "Christian nation"		The U.S. <u>should be</u> a "Christian nation"	
	Yes	No	Yes	No	Yes	No
	%	%	%	%	%	%
All U.S. adults	60	37	33	64	45	51
All Christians	69	28	30	67	62	35
Protestant	73	24	27	69	68	28
White evangelical	81	17	23	75	81	18
White, not evangelical	70	26	32	62	54	40
Black Protestant	57	37	26	68	65	30
Catholic	62	35	34	64	47	49
White Catholic	68	29	36	61	56	40
Hispanic Catholic	54	42	31	66	36	60
All non-Christians	44	54	40	58	16	81
Jewish*	36	64	55	44	16	84
Religiously unaffiliated	45	53	38	60	17	80
Atheist	25	74	41	59	6	94
Agnostic	38	61	46	53	8	91
Nothing in particular	53	45	34	63	23	72
Republican/lean Rep.	76	22	29	69	67	31
Democrat/lean Dem.	47	52	39	59	29	69
Ages 18-29	50	49	34	66	23	76
30-49	55	42	33	65	39	57
50-64	63	34	31	65	56	40
65+	73	23	36	59	63	33

* The survey included 123 interviews with Jewish respondents who were asked these questions, with an effective sample size of 61 and a 95% confidence level margin of error of plus or minus 12.5 percentage points. This margin of error conservatively assumes a reported percentage of 50%.
Note: Those who did not answer are not shown. White and Black adults include those who report being only one race and are not Hispanic. Hispanics are of any race.
Source: Survey conducted Sept. 13-18, 2022, among U.S. adults.
"45% of Americans Say U.S. Should Be a 'Christian Nation'"

PEW RESEARCH CENTER

Opposition to LGBTQ+ rights and reproductive freedom is central to this narrative. The Supreme Court's decision in Dobbs v. Jackson Women's Health Organization, which overturned Roe v. Wade, was framed as a significant victory for religious conservatives. However, MAGA politicians continue to claim that Christianity is being erased from public life. This argument is used to justify efforts to reintroduce school prayer, ban LGBTQ+ books, and pass laws restricting classroom discussions of gender and sexual identity. These actions are less about protecting religious freedom and more about enforcing conservative Christian values through legislation, undermining the constitutional principle of church-state separation.

Christian nationalism—the belief that the United States should be governed according to conservative Christian principles—has gained significant influence within the MAGA movement (Whitehead & Perry, 2020). This ideology promotes the false notion that America was founded as an explicitly Christian nation, often disregarding the Constitution's commitment to religious pluralism. Trump's enduring support among evangelical voters, despite his well-documented personal moral failings, reveals that religious identity within MAGA is more about cultural and political alignment than doctrinal consistency. As long as he positions himself as a fighter against secular liberalism, his conduct remains secondary to his perceived role in upholding conservative Christian power in American politics.

How Cultural Anxieties Distract from Economic Concerns

Working-class Americans who support MAGA have legitimate economic grievances—wage stagnation, deindustrialization, and corporate consolidation have all contributed to financial insecurity. However, rather than addressing these issues, right-wing media and politicians emphasize cultural battles, redirecting economic frustration into outrage over social issues. By focusing on perceived threats like immigration, LGBTQ+ rights, and "leftist indoctrination" in schools, conservative leaders deflect attention from economic policies that overwhelmingly benefit corporations and the wealthy.

This strategy is particularly effective because it shifts blame away from the structural causes of economic hardship. While Trump and Republican leaders passed massive tax cuts for corporations and the ultra-rich, Fox News and conservative radio flooded the airwaves with outrage over NFL players kneeling during the national anthem or universities supposedly being overrun by radical leftists (Brownstein, 2017). These cultural flashpoints consumed far more media attention than discussions about stagnant wages, rising healthcare costs, or declining job security. Instead of directing anger at corporate greed or policies that deepen inequality, MAGA supporters are encouraged to blame immigrants, LGBTQ+ activists, or college professors for their declining quality of life.

The manufactured outrage over "woke capitalism" further illustrates this economic misdirection. The term refers to companies adopting progressive social stances, such as supporting LGBTQ+ rights or racial justice initiatives, to appeal to socially conscious consumers or bolster their public image. Right-wing media frequently attack companies like Disney and Nike for these positions, claiming they betray American values. However, these same outlets rarely criticize such corporations for exploitative labor practices, tax avoidance, or excessive political lobbying—issues that significantly impact workers' lives (Hartzog & Stulberg, 2022). This selective outrage diverts attention from the deeper economic forces, including corporate influence over politics and the erosion of worker power.

By keeping voters focused on cultural battles, MAGA leaders can advance economic policies that primarily serve elites while maintaining the loyalty of a base that feels culturally under siege. The culture war is not merely a set of ideological grievances but a deliberate political strategy to preserve power. By framing progressivism as an existential threat, MAGA leaders ensure their base remains energized, even when their economic agenda fails to deliver material benefits. As long as cultural grievances continue to dominate conservative politics, meaningful debates about healthcare, wages, and labor rights will remain marginalized.

The Myth of Leftist Indoctrination in Public Schools

One of the central claims in the culture war narrative is that public schools serve as sites of leftist indoctrination, with educators allegedly imposing progressive ideologies on students. This narrative often targets discussions of race, gender, and sexuality, portraying teachers as "indoctrinating" children with leftist or "woke" ideas. However, there is little evidence to support these claims. Most K–12 public schools focus on delivering a well-rounded education, emphasizing core subjects like mathematics, science, history, and literature.

The myth of indoctrination typically relies on isolated incidents or exaggerated accounts, such as controversial guest speakers or specific lesson plans, to suggest a widespread crisis. Right-wing media often spotlight rare examples of teachers introducing political topics, like critical race theory (CRT) or LGBTQ+ rights, in the classroom. These cases are framed as proof of systemic indoctrination, despite representing a tiny fraction of educational activity. One frequently cited example involves a teacher in

California allegedly promoting a "woke" agenda by discussing LGBTQ+ rights with young students. However, such occurrences are outliers and do not reflect the broader reality of American classrooms (Klein, 2021). Nevertheless, these exceptions are weaponized by MAGA figures to stoke fear among conservative voters that their children are being subjected to leftist ideology.

Research and expert consensus affirm that educators' primary role is to foster critical thinking and expose students to a broad range of perspectives—an approach that has long been central to American public education. According to a 2021 National Education Association (NEA) report, public school teachers overwhelmingly focus on teaching foundational academic skills. Only a tiny percentage incorporate political or social topics into their lessons, and when they do, it is typically in the context of history, literature, or civic education (National Education Association, 2021).

Discussions of race and gender, for example, are usually introduced as part of established curricula, not as ideological instruction. These topics help students understand key historical events and social dynamics. Research shows that engaging with diverse perspectives strengthens students' critical thinking and increases empathy (Zhao, 2017). Far from indoctrination, exposure to multiple viewpoints encourages students to develop their own informed opinions.

Public opinion also reflects broad support for inclusive education. A 2021 Gallup poll found that most parents approve of age-appropriate discussions about historical injustice, racial inequality, and LGBTQ+ rights in public schools (Gallup, 2021). However, conservative political rhetoric often ignores these mainstream attitudes, focusing instead on claims that schools have become "indoctrination centers." This framing distracts from parents' real concerns, such as school funding, access to mental health services, and educational quality (Harris, 2020). By prioritizing culture war narratives over evidence-based issues, conservative leaders misrepresent the role of public education while sidelining the actual needs of students and families.

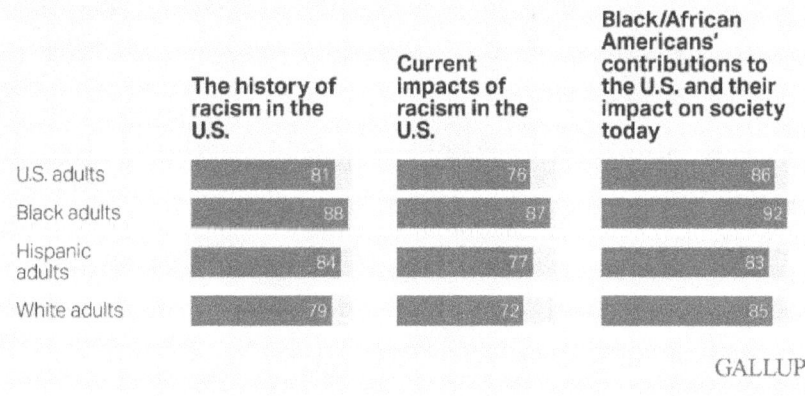

By framing public education as a battleground for political ideologies, MAGA figures and right-wing media have used fearmongering to rally their base, distract from substantive educational concerns, and manufacture a false sense of crisis. In 2021, for example, states like Florida and Texas passed laws restricting classroom discussions on race and gender, citing fears of "left-wing indoctrination"—despite little evidence to support such claims. This culture war rhetoric not only misrepresents the actual content of public education but also undermines schools' ability to prepare students for a diverse and interconnected world. According to the American Association of Colleges for Teacher Education (AACTE), the core mission of educators is to develop students' critical thinking skills, promote informed citizenship, and foster an understanding of diverse perspectives (AACTE, 2021). Achieving that goal often includes discussions of historical and contemporary social issues to help students navigate a complex, pluralistic society.

The MAGA movement's strategic use of the culture war has proven effective in mobilizing its base and consolidating political influence. By casting social and cultural issues, such as race, gender, and LGBTQ+ rights, as existential threats to American identity, MAGA has created a sense of urgency and victimhood among its supporters. Often fueled by moral panic and misinformation, this narrative deflects attention from more profound socioeconomic challenges, such as income inequality and stagnant wages. It also serves as a unifying force for a broad coalition of voters who feel unsettled by cultural and demographic changes.

At the heart of this culture war is the manipulation of emotion and grievance, tapping into fears of cultural displacement and the perceived erosion of traditional values. While MAGA's rhetoric echoes past political strategies, such as Nixon's "silent majority" and the Southern Strategy, it expands the battlefield to include a broader range of cultural and social issues. Through emotional appeals and a calculated focus on "wokeism," the movement has cultivated a political environment in which identity and values precede concrete policy outcomes.

This approach has profoundly shaped modern conservative politics and redefined the role of culture in the American political landscape. By focusing on divisive cultural issues, MAGA ensures its base remains engaged, even as economic and social problems persist. However, as the culture war continues to dominate political discourse, it is crucial to recognize how this strategy often obscures more urgent societal challenges and hinders meaningful dialogue on solutions that could address the root causes of inequality.

Key takeaways

- MAGA has weaponized cultural issues like race, gender, and LGBTQ+ rights to mobilize its base and shift focus from economic policy.

- Grievance politics reinforces the idea that traditional American values are under threat from progressive elites and social change.

- The strategy draws from Nixon's "silent majority" and the Southern Strategy, using identity and fear to maintain support.

- "Wokeism" and Critical Race Theory have been turned into political scare tactics, often through misinformation.

- The culture war distracts from deeper structural issues such as income inequality, corporate influence, and weakening labor rights.

- Christian nationalism plays a central role in framing MAGA's defense of "traditional values" and justifying legislative control over personal rights.

- The myth of leftist indoctrination in public schools is a political tool used to push censorship and deflect from underfunded education.

PART 03

DEBUNKING THE DECONTEXTUALIZED ARGUMENTS OF MAGA

CHAPTER EIGHT

The Economy Under Trump vs. Biden

Trump's narrative of economic success and Biden's alleged economic failures remain central to MAGA rhetoric. However, this argument selectively highlights favorable statistics while ignoring the broader economic context that shaped both presidencies. With continued job creation and GDP expansion, Trump inherited a growing economy from Obama. His administration's 2017 tax cuts provided a short-term boost but exacerbated wealth inequality and significantly increased the national deficit. In contrast, Biden assumed office amid an economy battered by the COVID-19 pandemic, global supply chain disruptions, and rising corporate profiteering. A meaningful evaluation of these claims requires a more profound analysis that moves beyond MAGA's oversimplified talking points. This section examines those claims in detail.

Claim: "Biden Caused Inflation"

The assertion that Biden's policies alone are directly responsible for the high inflation that peaked in 2022 is among the most misleading claims promoted by conservative media. While inflation is undoubtedly a significant issue affecting consumers, attributing it solely to the Biden administration overlooks the global and systemic factors contributing to its rise. This oversimplified explanation ignores key drivers, such as supply chain disruptions and geopolitical instability, and serves as a convenient political scapegoat for more profound, more complex economic challenges.

Context:

1. Inflation Was a Global Phenomenon

Inflation surged worldwide after the COVID-19 pandemic, affecting countries across the political and economic spectrum. The United States was not alone in experiencing price hikes—European nations, Canada, and other developed economies also faced significant inflation. This global trend was driven by several key factors: pandemic-related supply chain disruptions, a sharp rebound in consumer demand following lockdowns, and rising energy prices, which were further exacerbated by events such as Russia's invasion of Ukraine (International Monetary Fund [IMF], 2022).

While domestic policies can influence inflation, attributing it solely to Biden's economic agenda ignores the broader international context. Supply chain bottlenecks created shortages of essential goods—from microchips to food—driving prices higher across multiple sectors. Labor market disruptions, including worker shortages in critical industries, placed upward pressure on wages, further affecting consumer prices. At the same time, energy markets, already strained from pandemic-era volatility, were destabilized further by the war in Ukraine, which caused oil and gas prices to spike, increasing transportation and manufacturing costs globally. Central banks, including the Federal Reserve, responded by raising interest rates, but monetary policy alone could not fully mitigate these global supply-side challenges (Federal Reserve, 2022).

The tendency to blame Biden alone for inflation fails to account for these interconnected global dynamics. MAGA rhetoric focuses narrowly on U.S. policies, disregarding the fact that inflation was heavily influenced by external forces beyond any one administration's control. Moreover, economic data does not support the narrative that government spending under Biden was the primary cause of inflation. This points to more significant roles that supply-side constraints and global disruptions play. Notably, the same conservative critics who blame Biden were largely silent when similar inflation trends emerged in other countries with different fiscal policies, revealing the partisan nature of their arguments.

Reducing inflation to a political talking point distorts public understanding of economic policy. This misrepresentation shifts blame and creates unrealistic expectations about how quickly inflation can be controlled or what tools are available to address it. A serious response to inflation requires a multifaceted approach: stabilizing supply chains, curbing corporate price gouging, encouraging competitive markets, and investing in domestic production to reduce dependency on foreign sources. These solutions demand bipartisan engagement, yet MAGA's oversimplified narrative undermines any chance of substantive policy debate.

2. The Role of the American Rescue Plan

The $1.9 trillion American Rescue Plan (ARP), signed into law in March 2021, was designed as an emergency economic relief package in response to the devastating effects of the COVID-19 pandemic. Its primary goal was to mitigate the economic fallout of widespread shutdowns that had triggered soaring unemployment, financial insecurity, and severe disruptions to state and local government budgets. The ARP provided direct stimulus payments of up to $1,400 per person, extended enhanced unemployment benefits, increased funding for vaccine distribution, and allocated aid to small businesses struggling to survive. It also directed significant resources toward housing assistance, expanded the child tax credit, and supported school reopening efforts, ensuring that families and institutions could better weather the crisis (U.S. Congress, 2021).

Beyond immediate relief, the ARP aimed to prevent long-term economic scarring, which many economists feared could lead to a slow, uneven recovery similar to that following the 2008 financial crisis. Supporters of the plan—including progressive economists and Democratic policymakers—argued that robust intervention was essential to avoid mass evictions, business closures, and sustained joblessness. The child tax credit expansion alone reduced child poverty by nearly half in 2021, underscoring the plan's broad impact beyond short-term stabilization (Parolin et al., 2021).

Critics, particularly from the MAGA movement, argue that the ARP injected too much money into an economy already on the path to recovery, overstimulating demand and fueling inflation. They claim that stimulus checks and extended unemployment benefits increased consumer spending at a time when supply chains remained fragile, pushing prices higher. However, many economists contend that the ARP's contribution to inflation was modest relative to other major drivers, such as global supply chain disruptions, corporate price increases, and the Federal Reserve's monetary policy decisions (Blanchard, 2022). While former Treasury Secretary Larry Summers warned early on that the ARP's size could contribute to inflationary pressures (Summers, 2021), others—like Nobel laureate Paul Krugman—argued that the risks of under-stimulating the economy, and thus repeating the sluggish recovery of the 2010s, were far more dangerous (Krugman, 2021).

Despite the criticism, the ARP played a vital role in accelerating the post-pandemic recovery. Unemployment dropped from 6.2% in March 2021 to 3.9% by year's end (Bureau of Labor Statistics, 2022). The plan helped millions of families avoid financial ruin and provided essential funding to states and municipalities, preventing deep cuts to public services. The success of the vaccine rollout, which enabled businesses and schools to reopen safely, was also primarily funded by ARP provisions (Centers for Disease Control and Prevention, 2021). Studies suggest that, without the ARP's interventions, the U.S. economy could have faced a much slower, more painful recovery akin to the aftermath of the Great Recession (Bernstein, 2021).

Blaming the ARP as the leading cause of inflation oversimplifies a complex economic landscape. While it did increase demand, it also helped prevent a far more damaging downturn. Inflation was driven by a convergence of factors, including supply chain breakdowns, labor shortages, and global energy price spikes, many of which were outside the scope of domestic fiscal policy. Critics who frame the ARP as the primary cause of inflation often ignore the broader economic disruptions brought on by the pandemic and overlook the plan's critical role in averting a more profound economic crisis.

3. Corporate Profiteering and Price Gouging

Corporate behavior is a critical, yet often overlooked factor in discussions about inflation. While some arguments focus heavily on government spending as the root cause, they frequently ignore the significant role of corporate price-setting and profiteering. As the economy rebounded, major industries—including oil companies, food producers, and retail giants—raised prices far beyond their actual cost increases, leading to record-breaking profits. Many of these corporations, experiencing fewer operational disruptions than global supply chains, capitalized on inflationary conditions to expand their profit margins.

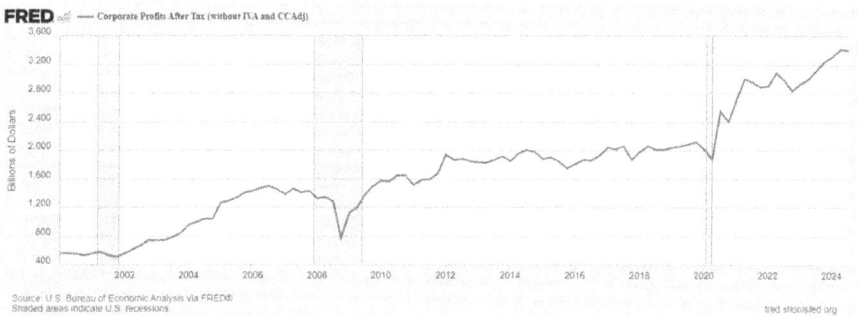

2021corporate profits contributed significantly to inflation, with markups accounting for more than half of the year's inflation rate. This suggests that many companies were not merely passing higher input costs to consumers but were actively increasing prices at a pace that exceeded those costs. For example, ExxonMobil and Chevron—two of the largest oil companies—reported unprecedented profits in 2022. ExxonMobil posted a net profit of $56 billion, marking a historic high for the Western oil industry. Chevron also recorded substantial earnings, reflecting a broader trend of soaring profits in the energy sector. Tyson Foods, a major meat producer, significantly raised its profit margins between 2021 and 2022 after increasing beef, pork, and chicken prices by more than 30%. Similarly, PepsiCo implemented widespread price hikes across its product lines to offset input costs, contributing to its strong financial performance during the same period.

Focusing solely on government spending as the primary driver of inflation overlooks the central role of corporate pricing strategies. Many businesses, prioritizing shareholder returns over consumer affordability, took advantage of global economic instability to boost their margins, substantially impacting household costs. Ignoring corporate profiteering in inflation debates presents a narrow and misleading picture, diverting attention from the private sector's substantial influence on price increases. Recognizing the multifaceted causes of inflation, including expanding corporate profits, is essential for crafting effective policies that manage inflation and protect consumers from exploitative pricing practices.

Claim: "Trump Had a Booming Economy Before COVID-19"

Trump frequently cites the pre-pandemic economy as one of his most outstanding achievements, often claiming that his policies created a booming economy. While it is true that, before COVID-19, the U.S. experienced low unemployment, a strong stock market, and steady GDP growth, these indicators were essentially the continuation of trends set in motion during the Obama administration. The economic recovery from the 2008 financial crisis was already well underway, with many foundational policies responsible for that growth implemented long before Trump took office.

To properly evaluate Trump's economic record, it is essential to consider the broader context. Many of the gains seen during his term were built on the momentum of the prior recovery. While his administration did implement policies, such as tax cuts and deregulation, that may have provided a short-term boost, those same policies also contributed to rising inequality and an expanding national deficit. A balanced assessment requires acknowledging the economy's inherited strengths and the longer-term consequences of Trump's economic agenda.

Context:

1. Trump Inherited a Strong Economy

Trump inherited an economy that was steadily recovering from the Great Recession, with many key indicators already on an upward trajectory. When he took office in January 2017, the U.S. was in the midst of its longest economic expansion in history—a recovery driven mainly by policies implemented under the Obama administration. These included the 2009 American Recovery and Reinvestment Act, which injected stimulus into the economy, and financial regulations that helped stabilize markets after the 2008 crisis.

By the time Trump assumed office, unemployment had fallen from its 2009 peak of 10% to just 4.7%, and job creation remained strong, averaging over 200,000 jobs per month in the final years of Obama's presidency (Federal Reserve, 2021). In comparison, during Trump's first three years, monthly job gains averaged approximately 182,000—still positive but slightly lower than under Obama's second term (BLS, 2020). Although Trump often claimed to have created a historic economic boom, the pace of job growth under his administration continued the momentum of an already robust labor market.

GDP growth under Trump followed a similar pattern of continuity rather than acceleration. His first three years saw an average annual growth rate of about 2.5%—comparable to Obama's second term and well below the 4% average during the Clinton administration in the late 1990s (BEA, 2020). Despite promises of sustained 3–4% growth, the 2017 Tax Cuts and Jobs Act did not deliver on that projection. While the corporate tax cuts led to a short-term boost in equity markets, they resulted primarily in stock buybacks rather than significant wage increases or capital investment (CBO, 2019).

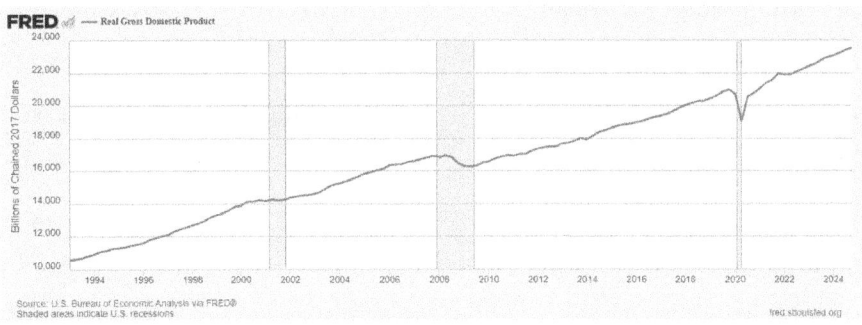

Trump's frequent claim that he built "the greatest economy in history" overlooks that many of the economic gains he highlighted resulted from a decade-long recovery that predated his presidency. Although the stock market reached record highs under his administration, stock market performance is not a comprehensive measure of economic health, mainly because market wealth is disproportionately concentrated among the wealthiest Americans.

Economic growth, job creation, and wage increases during Trump's presidency generally mirrored pre-existing trends rather than reflecting an unprecedented surge. Ultimately, Trump presided over the later phase of expansion, which was already in progress. While his policies—particularly tax cuts and deregulation—may have influenced certain areas of the economy, they did not fundamentally alter its trajectory. Understanding this context is essential to accurately evaluating the true nature of the economy during Trump's time in office.

2. The 2017 Tax Cuts: Short-Term Boost, Long-Term Problems

Trump's 2017 Tax Cuts and Jobs Act (TCJA) was a signature economic policy aimed at stimulating growth by reducing corporate tax rates and providing temporary relief to middle-class Americans. The law lowered the corporate tax rate from 35% to 21%—one of the most significant reductions in U.S. history—and included individual tax cuts set to expire in 2025. While proponents argued the cuts would benefit all Americans, data shows that the primary beneficiaries were wealthy individuals, large corporations, and their shareholders. The top 1% of earners received a disproportionate share of the benefits, while middle- and lower-income families saw only modest and temporary gains (Tax Policy Center, 2018). In contrast, corporations received permanent tax reductions, ensuring their benefits would far outlast those of average Americans.

The tax cuts in theory were meant to encourage business investment, economic expansion, and wage growth. In practice, however, many corporations used their tax windfalls for stock buybacks instead of expanding operations or raising wages (Zucman & Saez, 2020). In 2018 alone, corporations spent over $1 trillion on stock buybacks, prioritizing shareholder value over worker compensation (Reuters, 2019). This strategy disproportionately benefited executives and wealthy investors, as inflated share prices led to more significant executive bonuses and increased wealth concentration.

Trump and Republican lawmakers claimed the corporate tax cuts would boost wages by an average of $4,000 per worker, yet wage growth remained relatively stagnant while corporate profits soared (Bivens & Mishel, 2019). According to the Economic Policy Institute, most tax cut benefits flowed to the highest income brackets and corporate stakeholders, exacerbating income inequality . Companies sometimes followed their buybacks with mass layoffs, contradicting the claim that tax cuts would lead to job creation.

For example, in late 2018, General Motors (GM) announced stock buybacks while simultaneously closing several factories and laying off thousands of workers, despite benefiting from the tax cuts. After receiving billions in tax savings, AT&T cut over 40,000 jobs instead of expanding its workforce or raising wages. These cases highlight how the tax cuts failed to deliver on promises of economic growth and job creation, instead reinforcing a trend of prioritizing short-term shareholder gains over long-term investment and worker well-being.

Beyond concerns about inequality, the tax cuts had significant fiscal consequences. Despite claims that the TCJA would "pay for itself" through economic growth, the outcome was markedly different. The Congressional Budget Office (CBO) estimated the law would add nearly $2 trillion to the national deficit over a decade (CBO, 2019). By 2019, the annual federal deficit had grown by almost 50% compared to 2016, even before pandemic-related emergency spending (CBO, 2020). This surge in debt limited future fiscal flexibility, making it harder to fund infrastructure, social programs, and other essential investments.

While Trump frequently touted the pre-pandemic economy as one of his most significant accomplishments, his economic policies were built mainly on the recovery initiated under the Obama administration. By the time Trump took office, the economy was already experiencing steady growth, low unemployment, and rising markets thanks to post-recession policy measures. The TCJA provided a temporary boost but failed to deliver long-term structural improvements in wages, mobility, or fiscal responsibility. Rather than fostering broad-based prosperity, the tax cuts deepened income inequality, disproportionately benefited the wealthy, and strained the federal budget. Framing the tax cuts as an unqualified success oversimplifies economic reality and ignores the more profound systemic challenges facing American workers and the nation's fiscal health.

Claim: "Biden's Economy Is a Disaster"

MAGA rhetoric frequently portrays Biden's economic record in dire terms, claiming his policies have led to widespread economic failure. While it is true that the U.S. has faced significant challenges under his administration, particularly rising inflation, Biden's overall economic performance is far more nuanced and resilient than such claims suggest. His administration has made notable progress in rebuilding the economy, with strong growth in key areas such as job creation, manufacturing, and infrastructure investment.

Context:

1. Job Growth and Unemployment

Biden's first two years in office saw record job creation, with over 12 million jobs added, outpacing job growth under any recent president (BLS, 2023). While some of this growth resulted from the natural rebound following the COVID-19 pandemic, Biden's policies also played a key role. Infrastructure, clean energy, and industrial policy investments helped create jobs across multiple sectors.

Notably, the 2021 Infrastructure Investment and Jobs Act allocated $1.2 trillion to modernize the nation's infrastructure, including roads, bridges, public transit, and clean energy—critical components of long-term economic development (White House, 2021). Biden's administration also prioritized domestic manufacturing through initiatives like the CHIPS and Science Act, which aims to bring semiconductor production back to the U.S. and reduce reliance on Taiwan, making that sector more resistant to Chinese aggression in the region. These efforts are not only about immediate recovery—they are part of a broader strategy to build long-term economic resilience.

By early 2023, unemployment had dropped to 3.4%—the lowest level in 50 years—signaling a strong labor market recovery (BLS, 2023). This milestone was not simply the result of post-pandemic momentum; it reflected the impact of Biden's targeted fiscal policies. His administration's focus on clean energy and green jobs has also opened up new employment opportunities, making job growth robust and more sustainable.

Wage growth, particularly for lower-income workers, has been another priority. Biden's economic agenda has supported collective bargaining and wage increases, addressing long-standing problems like wage stagnation and income inequality, which were largely ignored during Trump's presidency.

2. Manufacturing Growth and Infrastructure Investment

Biden's approach starkly contrasts with Trump's economic strategy, which centered on tax cuts and deregulation measures that offered short-term boosts but failed to address deeper systemic issues such as wage inequality and reliance on foreign manufacturing. Under Trump, the 2017 Tax Cuts and Jobs Act (TCJA) delivered significant tax breaks for corporations and the wealthy but did little to tackle the U.S. economy's long-term structural problems. The cuts disproportionately benefited the rich, with many corporations using their windfalls for stock buybacks rather than expanding operations or raising wages (Zucman & Saez, 2020). In contrast, Biden's policies focus on investments to build a more resilient and equitable economy, emphasizing sustainable growth through infrastructure development, clean energy, and domestic manufacturing.

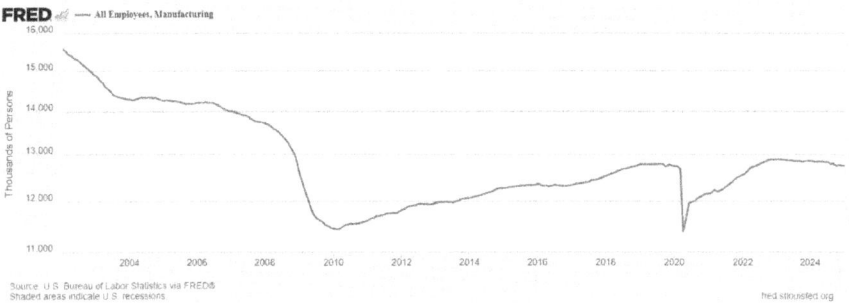

MAGA rhetoric often ignores the context in which Biden inherited the economy. Unlike Trump, who entered office during a steady recovery from the Great Recession, Biden took office amid a global health crisis, widespread economic disruption, and unprecedented supply chain challenges. The pandemic had left deep scars on the labor market, global inflation was mounting, and economic uncertainty was widespread. Comparing the two administrations without considering these vastly different starting points oversimplifies the complexity of the economic landscape and distorts the reality of their respective challenges.

The more relevant question is not who presided over the "better" economy, but which set of policies is more likely to generate long-term, inclusive prosperity. Trump's tax cuts and deregulation lifted corporate profits and the stock market but did little to reverse wage stagnation or reduce income inequality. Biden's policies, in contrast, are structured around long-term investments in infrastructure, green technology, and advanced manufacturing initiatives that may take time to bear fruit but are aimed at building a more stable and sustainable economic foundation.

These investments target the American workforce, aiming to create high-paying, future-focused jobs in construction, renewable energy, and technology sectors. The strategy prioritizes broad-based growth over short-term market gains, offering a path toward a more inclusive and resilient economy.

While MAGA's criticisms of Biden's economic record are often designed to stoke division and oversimplify complex realities, a closer examination reveals that Biden's economic agenda focuses more on durable, long-term outcomes. Rather than relying on temporary boosts, his administration invests in the building blocks of economic stability and shared prosperity. By prioritizing infrastructure, manufacturing, and wage growth, Biden's approach aims to lay a strong foundation for future generations—something Trump's short-term, profit-driven policies largely failed to deliver. The real challenge is choosing a path that fosters an economy built to last, and Biden's strategy is better equipped to meet that challenge.

Key takeaways

- Trump's pre-COVID economic growth largely continued trends started under Obama; his tax cuts benefited the wealthy and worsened the deficit.

- Inflation under Biden was part of a global trend driven by supply chain issues, the war in Ukraine, and corporate profiteering—not just U.S. policies.

- The American Rescue Plan helped avoid economic collapse, supported millions, and contributed only modestly to inflation.

- Corporate profiteering during inflationary periods often went unaddressed in MAGA rhetoric, despite major impacts on prices.

- Trump's tax cuts failed to deliver lasting wage growth or job creation and increased inequality.

- Biden's economic policies emphasize infrastructure, green jobs, and manufacturing, focusing on long-term growth and resilience.

- Claims of economic disaster under Biden ignore record job creation, falling unemployment, and targeted investments in future industries.

CHAPTER NINE
Immigration

Facts vs. Fear

Few issues have defined the MAGA movement as strongly as immigration. Donald Trump built much of his political identity on hardline immigration policies, portraying migrants, especially those from Latin America, as threats to American jobs, safety, and culture. His policies and rhetoric fueled a sense of crisis, often blaming immigrants for the nation's problems. However, many arguments to justify these policies lack critical context. For instance, the claim that Obama deported more people than Trump ignores key differences in deportation strategies and the human rights violations under Trump's administration. Likewise, the assertion that Biden's policies have created "open borders" overlooks the complexities of the immigration system and the global factors driving migration. This chapter breaks down these key claims to better understand immigration policy and its impact on the U.S. economy and society.

Claim: "Obama Deported More People Than Trump"

A frequent defense of Trump's immigration record is the claim that Barack Obama deported more people than Trump. While technically accurate in raw numbers, this comparison is misleading because it ignores significant differences in enforcement priorities, methods, and definitions of deportation.

Context: The Changing Definition of "Deportation"

The claim originates from data provided by Immigration and Customs Enforcement (ICE) and Customs and Border Protection (CBP). Between 2009 and 2016, Obama oversaw approximately 3 million deportations, compared to about 1.8 million under Trump from 2017 to 2020 (Pew Research Center, 2021). However, those numbers require crucial context.

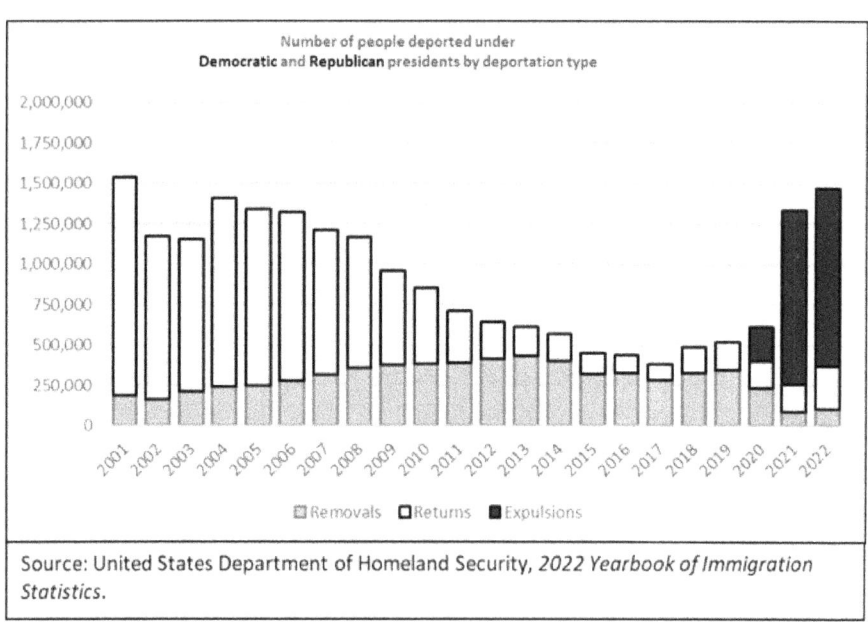

Under Obama, many deportations classified as "removals" included people caught at the border. A removal is an official deportation that carries legal penalties if the individual attempts to reenter. A "return," on the other hand, involves sending someone back without a formal deportation order, often immediately after a border apprehension. "Expulsions" are rapid removals under emergency measures, such as Title 42 during the COVID-19 pandemic, bypassing standard legal proceedings.

A counting change implemented during the Bush administration included border apprehensions in deportation statistics, which inflated Obama's numbers (Rosenblum & Meissner, 2014). Since many of these were quick turnarounds rather than complete legal deportations, they artificially increased the total under Obama. In contrast, Trump focused more heavily on interior enforcement and, later, Title 42 expulsions. This difference in enforcement approach and statistical methodology makes direct comparisons misleading.

Obama's enforcement also became more targeted over time. While he initially took a tough stance, his administration later prioritized deporting recent arrivals and individuals with criminal records, rather than long-term undocumented residents. Policies like Deferred Action for Childhood Arrivals (DACA) exemplified this shift, offering temporary protection to undocumented immigrants brought to the U.S. as children (American Immigration Council, 2019).

Trump, in contrast, expanded deportation priorities to include a much broader range of undocumented immigrants, including long-time residents with no criminal records. His administration's aggressive interior enforcement led to widespread fear in immigrant communities and included controversial practices such as family separations (Nowrasteh, 2020). While Obama's numbers may have been higher, Trump's approach was far more expansive and punitive.

Ultimately, the claim that Obama deported more people than Trump is an oversimplified talking point that fails to reflect the harshness and broader scope of Trump's immigration policies.

Claim: "Biden Has Open Borders"

Since taking office, Joe Biden has been repeatedly accused by MAGA supporters of pursuing an "open borders" policy—allegedly allowing unchecked migration into the United States. This claim has become central to MAGA rhetoric, framing Biden's approach as reckless and harmful to national security. However, this narrative is misleading and lacks nuance.

Context: Record Border Encounters and Global Migration Trends

The U.S. has experienced a record number of border encounters under Biden. In fiscal year 2022, U.S. Customs and Border Protection (CBP) recorded 2.3 million encounters at the southern border—the highest in U.S. history (CBP, 2023). However, equating this rise in encounters with "open borders" is misleading. High encounter numbers do not indicate a lack of enforcement or a policy of unrestricted migration; instead, they reflect a complex mix of factors, including increased global migration and the ongoing effects of existing U.S. border policies.

The term "encounters" is frequently misrepresented. Many individuals apprehended at the border are repeat crossers, meaning the number of unique migrants is lower than the raw data implies. Additionally, many of these encounters result in immediate expulsion or detention, not entry into the country. It is also important to note that migration surges have occurred under multiple administrations. Obama faced a spike in unaccompanied minors in 2014, and Trump dealt with migrant caravans and record asylum backlogs. Global conditions and long-term trends shape migration, not the policies of any single president.

1. Many Migrants Were Expelled Under Trump-era policies

Contrary to claims that Biden dismantled Trump's immigration framework, he retained several key policies, most notably Title 42, a public health order used under Trump to quickly expel migrants without processing asylum claims. Under Biden, more than 2.5 million migrants were expelled via Title 42 before it was lifted in 2023 (American Immigration Council, 2023). This policy allowed the government to bypass standard asylum procedures, meaning many migrant encounters under Biden ended in expulsion, not entry. That fact directly challenges the "open borders" narrative. If Biden had honestly pursued open borders, his administration would not have continued Title 42 expulsions for over two years.

Title 42 was lifted in May 2023, not because of a policy shift, but because the COVID-19 public health emergency officially ended. The policy had been justified as a pandemic-related measure, and once that justification expired, so did its legal standing. In its place, the administration implemented a stricter asylum rule under Title 8, which imposes harsher penalties, including a five-year reentry ban for those who cross illegally. This transition, rather than embracing open borders, signaled a return to formal immigration law enforcement.

Biden has also continued interior enforcement efforts, resulting in over 142,000 deportations in fiscal year 2023 (Department of Homeland Security, 2023). While Trump favored sweeping raids and broad deportation goals, Biden's approach has been more targeted, focusing on individuals with criminal records. Still, the administration has drawn criticism from both sides—immigration advocates who view the policies as too harsh, and conservatives who argue they are too lenient. Biden has sought a middle path, balancing enforcement with humanitarian considerations. His administration neither promotes open borders nor replicates Trump's mass deportation strategy.

2. Global Factors Driving Migration

The increase in border encounters during Biden's presidency cannot be attributed solely to U.S. policies. Global factors have played a significant role in driving migration trends. Political instability, climate change, and economic downturns—worsened by the COVID-19 pandemic—have triggered migration surges across multiple regions, including Latin America and Europe (United Nations, 2022).

Venezuela's economic collapse, fueled by hyperinflation and government mismanagement, has created one of the world's most significant displacement crises, forcing millions to flee. Gang violence and political instability in Central America—particularly in El Salvador, Honduras, and Guatemala—continue to push people north. In Haiti, extreme poverty, political chaos, natural disasters, and rampant gang violence have further deteriorated living conditions. These crises have generated a humanitarian emergency far beyond U.S. border policy.

Similarly, Russia's invasion of Ukraine has displaced millions, with many seeking asylum through legal U.S. immigration channels. The Biden administration responded by granting Temporary Protected Status (TPS) to Ukrainians, allowing them to remain in the U.S. rather than return to a war zone. Climate change has also fueled migration, particularly in regions where extreme weather has devastated agriculture and infrastructure. Prolonged droughts in Central America have led to food shortages, while hurricanes and flooding in the Caribbean have displaced entire communities. These climate-driven displacements underscore that the rise in border encounters stems from worsening global conditions, not merely changes in U.S. immigration policy.

Blaming Biden alone for these migration trends oversimplifies a complex reality. People are fleeing violence, poverty, and environmental collapse, not just responding to U.S. policies. While immigration policy affects how migrants are processed at the border, it does not control the forces driving them to flee. No single administration can dictate global migration flows. Any serious discussion must consider these external factors rather than reduce the issue to partisan talking points. Effectively addressing migration requires international cooperation, economic investment in crisis-prone regions, and policies that balance border security with humanitarian responsibility.

3. Biden's Tougher Stance on Illegal Crossings

Contrary to claims of "open borders," the Biden administration has implemented stricter measures to deter illegal crossings. While expanding legal pathways for migration, such as refugee admissions, family reunification, and humanitarian parole, Biden has also tightened asylum eligibility requirements.

New policies require migrants to seek asylum in another country before reaching the U.S. border, mirroring Trump-era "safe third country" agreements. Additional regulations make it more difficult for those who cross the border illegally to claim asylum unless they meet strict criteria (Krogstad, 2023). These measures have drawn criticism from immigrant advocates, who argue that they echo some of Trump's most restrictive immigration policies.

Biden has also expanded cooperation with Mexico to curb migration. Agreements with Mexican authorities have led to increased enforcement on their side of the border, reducing the number of migrants reaching the U.S. in the first place. This approach reflects strategic enforcement, not a relaxation of border control.

While it is true that border encounters have increased under Biden, the claim that he has enacted "open borders" is inaccurate. Immigration enforcement remains in place, though the administration's strategy emphasizes legal migration pathways and focuses deportation efforts on individuals who do not qualify for asylum. Rather than signaling a lack of control, Biden's approach represents a more nuanced effort to address humanitarian needs and enforcement priorities.

The "open borders" rhetoric ignores the complex and multifaceted nature of U.S. immigration policy. Biden's strategy seeks to balance security with compassion, providing legal options for migrants while maintaining firm enforcement measures for those who do not follow lawful channels.

Claim: "Immigrants Take American Jobs"

A persistent argument within the MAGA movement claims that immigrants, especially undocumented ones, take jobs from American workers and suppress wages. This idea has been used for decades to justify restrictive immigration policies, drawing more on economic fears than factual analysis. However, the claim oversimplifies the labor market, ignores the broader economic contributions of immigrants, and overlooks the role of corporate profit-driven strategies in shaping employment conditions and wages.

Context: The Economic Impact of Immigration

Economists widely refute the belief that immigrants harm the job market. Research consistently shows that both legal and undocumented immigrants provide a net positive contribution to the economy. Immigrants fill critical labor shortages, contribute to innovation, and increase consumer demand across various sectors, fostering overall economic growth (Peri, 2020). Rather than displacing American workers, immigrants help sustain industries, increase competitiveness, and support business operations. The economic dynamism fueled by immigration bolsters the country's global standing, prevents stagnation, and promotes resilience.

1. Undocumented Workers and the Labor Market

Undocumented immigrants primarily work in industries that struggle to attract native-born workers, such as agriculture, construction, and food services. These sectors rely heavily on immigrant labor, as the jobs are often physically demanding, low-paying, and subject to inconsistent employment conditions. A study by the National Bureau of Economic Research found that undocumented workers tend to complement rather than compete with native-born workers. Their participation enables business expansion, increasing the number of jobs available to American workers (Orrenius & Zavodny, 2019). Without this labor force, entire industries—especially farming and food production—would face severe challenges, likely resulting in higher consumer prices and reduced economic output.

Additionally, many undocumented immigrants fill jobs in sectors where labor shortages persist because wages are kept low to maximize corporate profits. If businesses were required to rely solely on American workers, they would either need to raise wages, cut profits, and raise consumer prices, or outsource labor to countries with lower costs. In this context, immigrant labor does not "steal" jobs; it enables American industries to remain competitive in global markets. Without access to this workforce, companies would be more likely to move operations overseas, leading to job losses for American workers.

2. Wages and Job Competition

While some argue that immigration lowers wages for native-born workers, particularly in low-skilled jobs, economic research does not strongly support this claim. Any wage suppression linked to immigration is typically short-term and minimal, often offset by broader economic expansion. Many studies indicate that immigration can lead to long-term wage growth by diversifying the labor force and boosting productivity (Card, 2009). The modest wage effects observed in specific industries are often exaggerated to fuel anti-immigrant rhetoric. In contrast, more significant drivers of wage stagnation—such as corporate wage suppression, declining union power, and automation—are routinely ignored.

Moreover, reducing immigration would not necessarily raise wages for native-born workers. A labor shortage would increase agriculture and food production costs, ultimately increasing consumer prices. Rather than benefiting American workers, such policies could make essential goods more expensive and incentivize companies to relocate operations abroad for cheaper labor. This reality underscores the interdependence of labor markets and economic policy, revealing that simplistic narratives about job competition fail to capture the broader economic picture.

3. The Demographic Reality

The U.S. faces a growing demographic challenge as its population ages and birth rates decline. With the retirement of the baby boomer generation, pressure is mounting on the workforce and social support systems. Fewer young people are entering the labor market, and this shrinking workforce threatens long-term economic stability by slowing growth and reducing the ability to support an increasingly dependent population.

Immigrants help mitigate this burden by filling labor shortages in critical sectors and contributing to programs like Social Security and Medicare. They often pay taxes without comparable benefits and help sustain public services. According to the National Academy of Sciences (2017), immigrants significantly bolster the U.S. economy and are key to maintaining the viability of essential social programs. Without immigration, the tax base would contract, leading to fiscal strain, reduced services, or increased taxes on the remaining workforce.

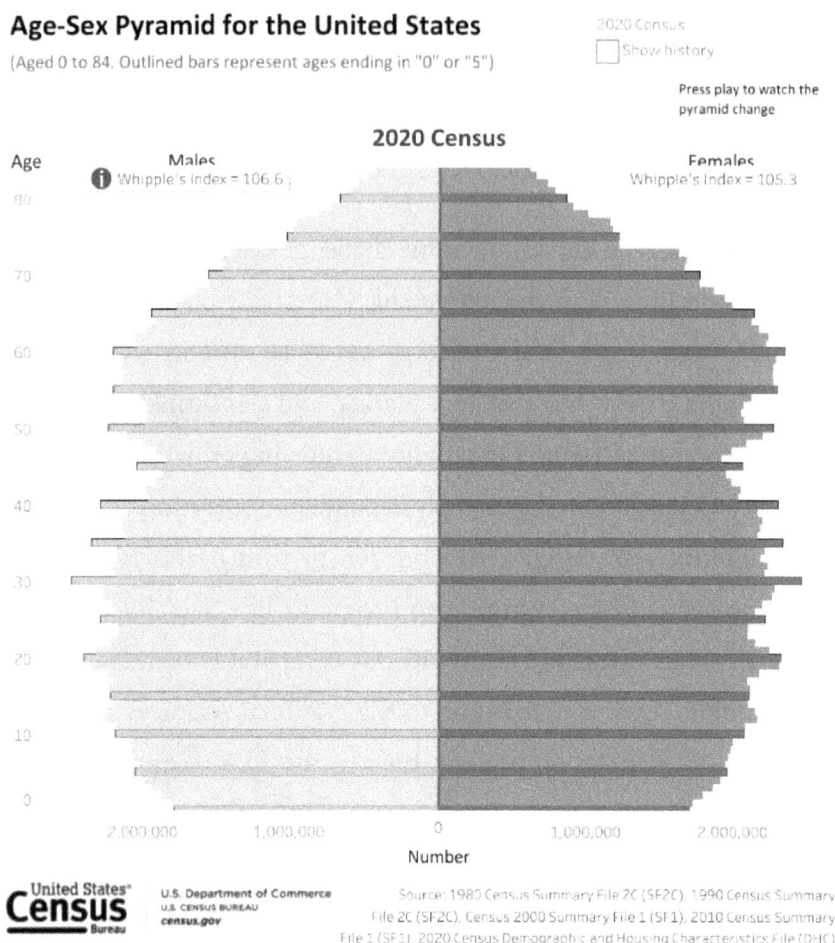

Restricting immigration would narrow the labor pool needed to support an aging population. Key industries such as healthcare, elder care, and agriculture are already experiencing acute labor shortages. The demand for healthcare workers—including nurses and home health aides—continues to outpace supply, with many positions remaining unfilled due to a lack of domestic applicants. Immigrants are essential to sustaining these sectors and, by extension, the broader economy.

Limiting immigration will only deepen the labor shortfall, slow economic growth, and strain vital services. The argument that immigration harms American workers overlooks the reality that immigrant labor is central to economic resilience, especially as the native-born workforce shrinks. Without enough workers, maintaining the current standard of living or expanding economic opportunity will become increasingly difficult.

The real threat to economic stability is not immigration but the demographic pressures of an aging population and a declining birth rate. Immigrants are a vital part of the solution to this crisis.

Economic research does not support the claim that immigrants take jobs from Americans. On the contrary, legal and undocumented immigrants play a critical role in maintaining the U.S. economy. While MAGA rhetoric relies on selective data and misleading narratives, the facts show that immigrants fill essential roles, contribute to growth, and help preserve the nation's global competitiveness.

Portraying immigrants as a threat to jobs and wages ignores their broader economic contributions and obscures the structural causes of wage stagnation. Moving beyond this rhetoric requires a more informed, evidence-based approach to immigration policy that aligns economic needs with national security and humanitarian values. Unfortunately, the MAGA movement's reliance on fear-driven narratives makes it harder to pursue meaningful reforms. To secure long-term economic prosperity, the U.S. must adopt a comprehensive strategy recognizing immigrants as indispensable to the labor force and the nation's future.

Key takeaways

- Comparing deportation numbers between Obama and Trump ignores changes in definitions, enforcement focus, and human rights practices.

- The "open borders" accusation against Biden is misleading; he retained and expanded enforcement tools like Title 42 and Title 8.

- Rising border encounters reflect global migration crises, not a lack of U.S. enforcement.

- MAGA narratives overlook Biden's targeted enforcement and efforts to create legal immigration pathways.

- Immigrants, including undocumented workers, support essential industries and economic growth rather than taking jobs from Americans.

- Restricting immigration would worsen labor shortages, reduce economic resilience, and accelerate demographic decline.

- A nuanced, evidence-based approach is needed, but fear-based rhetoric blocks progress toward real reform.

Chapter Ten
Law and Order

Crime, Protests, and Policing

MAGA rhetoric claims that crime has spiraled out of control under Joe Biden, blaming Democratic policies for rising violence and accusing progressive leaders of abandoning public safety. Right-wing media amplify this narrative by spotlighting violent crime in major cities, particularly those led by Democratic mayors, as supposed proof that liberal governance fuels lawlessness. A central element of this argument is the misleading claim that Democrats broadly support "defunding the police," a distortion that ignores the fact that most mainstream Democratic policies focus on reform, not abolition. This narrative is designed to stoke fear and position MAGA-aligned Republicans as the only defenders of public safety.

However, these claims do not hold up under scrutiny. While violent crime did rise sharply in 2020, that surge began under Donald Trump, not Biden. The increase was driven by a complex mix of factors, including the COVID-19 pandemic, economic instability, and a record-breaking surge in gun sales, not by Democratic policy. Crime trends have shifted significantly recently, with violent crime declining in many cities by 2023.

The MAGA narrative selectively highlights statistics from cities like Chicago, New York, and Los Angeles while ignoring Republican-led states with some of the highest per capita violent crime rates, such as Louisiana and Mississippi. This cherry-picking of data creates a false impression that Democratic leadership inherently results in lawlessness, while disregarding broader national crime trends.

Claim: "Crime Skyrocketed Under Biden"

MAGA supporters argue that crime has surged since Joe Biden took office, blaming the rise in violence on Democratic policies. They claim that progressive criminal justice reforms, lenient prosecution, and reduced policing have emboldened criminals, leading to lawlessness and widespread social unrest. Right-wing media frequently highlight violent incidents in major cities, particularly those led by Democrats, as evidence that liberal leadership has made communities more dangerous.

A central theme of this narrative is the claim that under Biden, criminals face fewer consequences, allowing crime to flourish. Conservative pundits cite policies such as bail reform, efforts to reduce prison populations, and the "defund the police" movement as proof that Democrats have abandoned public safety.

However, these arguments collapse under scrutiny. Crime trends are shaped by a complex web of social, economic, and systemic factors, many of which extend beyond the influence of any single presidential administration. Historical data shows that the rise in violent crime began before Biden took office, and crime rates have declined in many areas since then.

Context:

Crime Spiked in 2020—Under Trump

Donald Trump and his allies frequently assert that crime has surged under Biden, but a closer examination of the data reveals a more nuanced picture. While violent crime did increase sharply in 2020, that surge began while Trump was still in office. The U.S. murder rate rose by approximately 30% in 2020—the most significant single-year increase in modern American history (FBI, 2021). If crime trends were solely attributable to presidential leadership, this spike would reflect Trump's presidency, not Biden's.

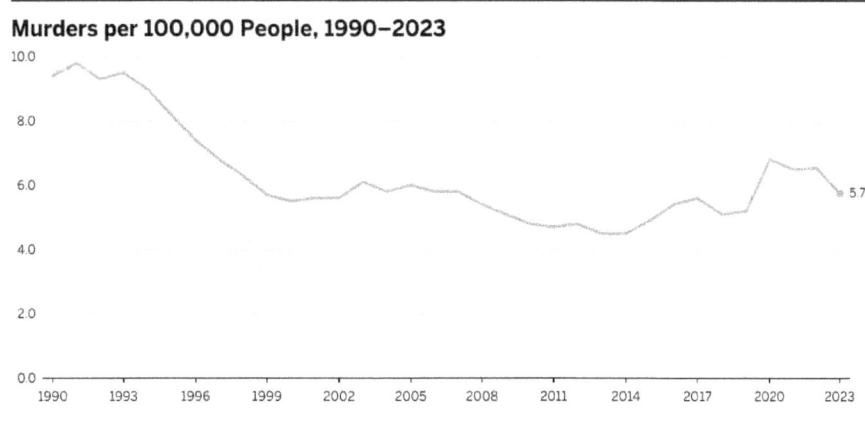

Source: Uniform Crime Reporting Program. Crime in the United States Estimations, 2020, 2022, 2023: Table 1.

The 2020 crime surge was driven by multiple overlapping crises, most notably the COVID-19 pandemic. The pandemic created extreme social and economic instability, increasing stress, unemployment, and social isolation—conditions long associated with higher crime rates (Rosenfeld et al., 2021). Lockdowns and disruptions to daily life reduced access to social services, strained mental health resources, and heightened domestic tensions, all contributing to the rise in violence.

Gun sales also soared during this period, further exacerbating violent crime rates. In 2020 alone, nearly 23 million firearms were purchased—a 64% increase from the previous year (Small Arms Survey, 2021). Research consistently shows that increased gun circulation leads to higher levels of gun violence. The unprecedented surge in firearm purchases significantly contributed to the rise in homicides. Many of these weapons were acquired by first-time gun owners with little or no training, increasing the likelihood of fatal encounters.

Studies have established a direct link between gun availability and firearm-related deaths, including both homicides and suicides (Cook & Goss, 2020). Additionally, states with higher gun ownership rates tend to experience significantly more firearm homicides, suggesting that more guns inherently increase the risk of lethal violence (Siegel et al., 2013). The combination of heightened social tensions, economic instability, and record-breaking gun sales created conditions ripe for a surge in firearm-related crime.

Another critical factor was the shift in policing strategies following the George Floyd protests. Some law enforcement agencies reported a decline in proactive policing—often called "de-policing"—as officers became more hesitant to engage in aggressive enforcement due to increased scrutiny and strained community relations (Maguire et al., 2021). While MAGA narratives often blame the Black Lives Matter movement for emboldening criminals, the reality is more complex. While some local increases in crime may have been influenced by reduced police activity, this does not explain the nationwide rise in violent crime, which was primarily driven by broader societal disruptions.

Despite these well-documented causes, Trump and his supporters continue to cite the 2020 crime spike as proof of Democratic failure, ignoring the fact that these trends began under his administration. More importantly, they overlook that crime patterns have shifted significantly since Biden took office.

2. Crime Trends Under Biden

Despite persistent claims that crime has worsened under Biden, the data tell a different story. By mid-2023, homicides had dropped by 12% nationwide (FBI, 2023), significantly reversing the 2020 trend. Other categories of violent crime, including aggravated assault and robbery, also declined in many cities. While property crime increased slightly in some areas, overall crime rates remained well below historical highs.

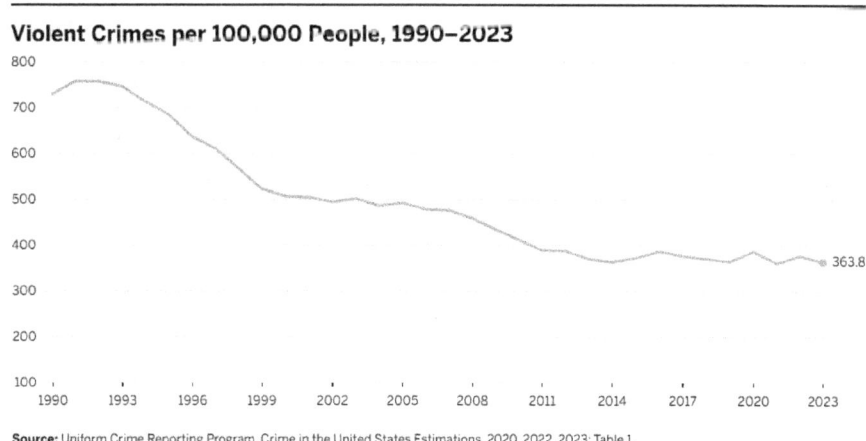

Source: Uniform Crime Reporting Program, Crime in the United States Estimations, 2020, 2022, 2023; Table 1.

MAGA rhetoric often relies on selectively presented statistics, focusing on short-term spikes in specific locations while ignoring broader downward trends. Right-wing media frequently highlight crime in cities like Chicago, New York, and Los Angeles, reinforcing the narrative that Democratic-led cities are descending into lawlessness. This framing omits key context. For instance, Chicago's homicide rate dropped by 13% in 2023 (Chicago Police Department, 2023); New York City saw a 10% decline in major crime categories during the first half of 2023 (NYPD, 2023); and Los Angeles reported a 17% reduction in homicides the same year (LAPD, 2023).

Meanwhile, Republican-led states like Louisiana and Mississippi continue to report the highest violent crime rates per capita (FBI, 2023), yet conservative media rarely acknowledge these figures. By focusing only on crime in Democratic strongholds, this selective framing creates a misleading perception that crime is a uniquely Democratic problem, when in fact it is a nationwide issue shaped by a complex interplay of economic, social, and policy-related factors.

Moreover, the claim that Biden's policies have fueled crime ignores the reality that today's crime rates remain significantly lower than in the 1990s, when violent crime in the U.S. peaked. Since 1991, the national crime rate has declined by nearly 50%, despite fluctuations in individual years (Bureau of Justice Statistics, 2023). This historical perspective is crucial, yet it is almost absent from MAGA narratives, which rely on cherry-picked data to stoke fear rather than present an accurate picture of crime trends in the United States.

Claim: "Democrats Want to Defund the Police"

Conservative critics argue that Democratic leaders have pushed to weaken policing, pointing to calls to "defund the police" as evidence of a broader effort to dismantle law enforcement. This claim suggests that Democratic policies have made communities less safe by reducing police funding and limiting officers' ability to do their jobs. However, this argument misrepresents both the intent behind policing reforms and the actual budget decisions made by Democratic-led cities.

Context:

1. What "Defund the Police" Actually Meant

The phrase "defund the police" became widely known during the 2020 George Floyd protests, but its meaning was often distorted and misunderstood. While some activists did call for the complete abolition of police departments, the broader movement focused on reallocating portions of police budgets toward other public safety initiatives. The goal was not to eliminate law enforcement but to rethink how public safety is funded, emphasizing strategies that prevent crime before it happens rather than relying solely on police intervention after the fact. Advocates argued that investing in mental health services, community-based violence prevention programs, and social services could reduce crime more effectively than increasing police budgets alone (Ray, 2020).

This approach was rooted in studies showing that police are often tasked with addressing issues, such as homelessness, drug addiction, and mental health crises, that they are not explicitly trained to handle. Proponents of reallocation believed that directing some funding toward professionals in these fields could lead to better outcomes and reduce unnecessary confrontations between police and civilians. Additionally, research has indicated that long-term crime prevention is more closely tied to economic opportunity, access to healthcare, and stable housing than the number of police officers in a given city. By investing in these areas, advocates argued that cities could lower crime rates without increasing aggressive policing tactics that disproportionately affect marginalized communities.

However, opponents seized on the slogan as evidence that Democrats wanted to abolish the police entirely—a characterization that was misleading but politically effective. Right-wing media and Republican politicians used the phrase to stoke fears of rising crime and social disorder, often ignoring the nuanced policy discussions behind the movement. This oversimplification allowed critics to paint all Democrats with the same broad brush, even though many within the party did not support the most radical interpretations of the slogan.

2. Did Democrats Defund the Police?

Despite repeated claims that Democrats have slashed police budgets and weakened law enforcement, the reality is quite different. While some cities made initial cuts to police funding in response to public pressure following the George Floyd protests, many later restored or even increased those budgets as concerns over crime grew. The broader trend has not been toward defunding, but rather maintaining or expanding law enforcement budgets, often alongside efforts to improve accountability and reform.

President Joe Biden has been particularly vocal in opposing calls to defund the police. Throughout his presidency, he has advocated for increased funding for law enforcement while pushing for reforms to improve accountability and community trust. In 2022, he signed the Bipartisan Safer Communities Act, which provided resources for law enforcement and funded community violence intervention programs to reduce crime through preventative measures (White House, 2022).

Similarly, major Democratic-led cities have not embraced widespread defunding. New York City, Los Angeles, and Chicago—often cited by critics as progressive governance examples—have increased police funding in recent years. In many cases, police budgets have grown beyond pre-2020 levels, directly contradicting claims that Democrats have systematically worked to dismantle law enforcement (Urban Institute, 2023). Even cities that initially reduced funding, such as Minneapolis and Seattle, eventually reversed course and reinvested in policing following public debates over crime and safety.

The disconnect between rhetoric and reality highlights how "defund the police" became more of a political weapon than an accurate description of policy changes. While some local governments did explore reallocating funds, there was never a coordinated Democratic effort to dismantle police departments nationwide. Instead, discussions around public safety have remained focused on balancing law enforcement funding with investments in crime prevention and community services. The claim that Democrats defunded the police is not only misleading—it also ignores the complexity of public safety policy and the ongoing efforts to build a more effective and accountable justice system.

Claim: "Crime Is a Problem in Democrat-Run Cities"

"Crime is more prevalent in cities governed by Democrats." This claim, frequently repeated by Trump and fellow Republicans, is used to suggest that progressive policies lead to lawlessness and disorder. It serves to justify calls for stricter policing and to frame Republicans as the true defenders of "law and order." However, crime trends do not follow a simple partisan pattern. Crime is a complex issue shaped by multiple factors—economic conditions, policing strategies, and broader societal trends—all of which extend well beyond the political affiliation of a city's leadership.

Moreover, many of the largest U.S. cities, where crime rates are naturally higher due to population density, have been Democratic strongholds for decades. This long-standing political alignment makes it misleading to suggest a direct causal link between party governance and crime. Additionally, Republican-led states consistently report some of the highest per-capita violent crime rates, further challenging the notion that Democratic leadership is the primary driver of criminal activity. Most importantly, crime patterns have evolved over decades and have been influenced by long-term economic changes, demographic shifts, and policies at multiple levels of government, not by the actions of a single president, governor, or mayor over a short period.

Context:

1. Crime Is a National Issue, Not a Partisan One

Attributing crime to Democratic leadership alone ignores the broader and more nuanced factors that influence crime nationwide. While urban areas do tend to experience higher crime rates, this has been true for decades, regardless of whether Democrats or Republicans lead those cities. Higher crime in cities primarily results from population density, economic inequality, and social challenges, not political party control. These conditions create environments where crime is statistically more likely, making city governance only one part of a much larger equation.

In reality, crime is deeply linked to economic and social variables that are often beyond the control of any one political party. Factors such as job losses, housing instability, and lack of access to mental health services all contribute to crime trends, yet broader national economic policies and entrenched structural inequities shape them. Crime trends tend to follow long-term cycles influenced by social and economic shifts, not short-term political decisions. Reducing crime to a partisan issue oversimplifies these complexities and distracts from meaningful solutions.

2. Red States Often Have Higher Violent Crime Rates

The claim that crime is concentrated in Democratic-run cities also ignores the fact that many Republican-led states consistently report higher rates of violent crime. In 2022, states such as Louisiana, Mississippi, Alabama, and Missouri—all governed by Republicans—were among those with the highest murder rates in the country (FBI, 2023). These states have long embraced tough-on-crime policies and Republican leadership at multiple levels, yet still struggle with pervasive violence. This reality undermines the assumption that conservative governance inherently leads to safer communities and highlights the need to examine deeper systemic causes.

Conversely, states often portrayed as crime-ridden by conservative media, such as New York and California, have lower per-capita violent crime rates than many Republican-led states. This discrepancy weakens the argument that Democratic leadership is to blame for high crime and instead points to broader factors such as poverty, unemployment, education disparities, and access to firearms. Many of the highest-crime areas in red states suffer from long-term economic decline, limited access to social services, and high levels of gun ownership—conditions that persist regardless of which party is in power.

3. Crime Is Concentrated in Certain Areas, Regardless of Political Leadership

Crime rates are disproportionately high in urban areas, but this is not unique to Democratic-run cities. Regardless of political leadership, large cities tend to have higher concentrations of poverty, greater economic inequality, and more significant social challenges, all of which contribute to elevated crime rates. Even in Republican-controlled states, most violent crime is concentrated in urban centers. For example, cities like Houston, Dallas, and Phoenix—located in red states—experience high levels of crime, much like Democratic-led cities such as Chicago or Los Angeles.

The narrative linking crime to Democratic policies ignores the reality that crime trends align more closely with urbanization, population density, and socio-economic conditions than with party affiliation. Moreover, many cities in Republican-led states are subject to state-level policies that override local priorities. While these cities may vote Democratic at the local level, they often operate under laws and regulations set by Republican state governments. This dynamic complicates the claim that crime in urban areas reflects only local leadership. It is misleading to suggest that mayors and city councils are solely responsible for crime trends when broader state-level decisions significantly shape public safety outcomes.

Furthermore, crime does not fluctuate dramatically with a single election cycle. The conditions that drive crime, economic downturns, educational disparities, and social instability develop over many years. While local and state leaders can influence public safety, their policies cannot instantly reverse long-standing structural issues. Attempts to blame crime spikes solely on one administration ignore the gradual nature of crime trends and the long-term forces that shape them.

4. Many Republican-Led Cities Face Similar Crime Issues

If Democratic policies were indeed the root cause of rising crime, then Republican-led cities should logically experience much lower crime rates. However, cities such as Miami and Jacksonville—both governed by Republican mayors—continue to face crime challenges similar to those in Democratic-led cities (Pew Research Center, 2023). The persistence of crime in these cities directly undermines the notion that it is uniquely tied to Democratic leadership or policies. Instead, it highlights that crime is a multifaceted issue shaped by a complex mix of social, economic, and political factors that cannot be reduced to partisan lines.

Moreover, many Republican-led states with high crime rates receive substantial federal funding for law enforcement, yet these investments have not produced significantly lower crime rates. This suggests that crime prevention is not simply a matter of increasing police budgets—it also requires addressing deeper social and economic problems. Research consistently shows that areas with high poverty and limited access to education tend to experience elevated crime, regardless of political leadership. A city's crime rate is shaped by its current administration and decades of underlying economic and social conditions.

The broader reality is that crime trends are influenced by a wide range of factors: economic instability, inadequate educational opportunities, social unrest, and law enforcement practices—all of which cut across party lines. The selective narrative promoted by the MAGA movement oversimplifies this complex issue to serve a divisive political agenda, ignoring the full spectrum of causes behind crime. This approach distracts from real, long-term solutions such as addressing systemic inequality, investing in underserved communities, and reforming policing practices.

Thus, the claim that crime is a uniquely "Democratic problem" is not supported by evidence. Crime is driven by broader societal trends and structural challenges, not merely the party affiliation of a city's leadership.

Furthermore, the broader "law and order" narrative pushed by the MAGA movement relies more on fear-based messaging than on facts. While violent crime did spike in 2020, this occurred under Trump's presidency and was primarily driven by the disruptions of the COVID-19 pandemic. Since then, crime rates have declined, further discrediting the argument that Biden's administration has fueled a national crime wave.

Similarly, the claim that Democrats defunded the police is demonstrably false. Most major cities have recently increased their law enforcement budgets, with police department funding reaching record highs in many Democratic-led areas. Despite Republican rhetoric, there has been no widespread movement by Democratic leadership to abolish or dismantle police forces in a way that explains national crime trends.

Framing crime as a partisan issue serves a clear political purpose: it allows Republicans to cast themselves as defenders of public safety while deflecting from the failures of their policies. Crime is a complex issue that demands evidence-based solutions, not misleading partisan attacks. Effectively addressing crime requires acknowledging the long-term economic, social, and structural forces, rather than assigning blame to a single political party or administration.

Key takeaways

- Violent crime spiked in 2020 during Trump's presidency due to COVID-19, economic stress, and a surge in gun sales.

- Crime has declined in many cities since 2021, contradicting

MAGA claims that Biden caused a crime wave.

- The "defund the police" slogan was often misrepresented; most Democrats support reform, not abolition.

- Biden and major Democratic cities have increased police funding while also investing in community safety programs.

- Republican-led states often have higher violent crime rates than Democrat-led cities, undermining partisan narratives.

- The MAGA crime narrative oversimplifies and politicizes a complex issue shaped by long-term economic and social factors.

Chapter Eleven
Election Fraud and the Big Lie

The claim that the 2020 presidential election was "stolen" from Donald Trump remains one of the most dangerous and persistent narratives within the MAGA movement. Despite overwhelming evidence debunking allegations of widespread voter fraud, Trump and his allies relentlessly pushed this falsehood, culminating in the violent attack on the U.S. Capitol on January 6, 2021. The so-called "Big Lie" has had far-reaching consequences: eroding public trust in the electoral system, fueling political extremism, and deepening partisan divides.

This chapter explores the origins of election fraud claims, the mechanisms that allowed misinformation to spread rapidly, and the real-world consequences of this unprecedented assault on American democracy. Understanding how these falsehoods took hold—and why they continue to resonate with millions—sheds light on the broader efforts to delegitimize democratic institutions, sow distrust in government, and justify restrictive voting laws under the guise of election security.

Claim: "The 2020 Election Was Stolen"

Allegations of widespread voter fraud became the defining grievance of Trump's post-election narrative. From the moment major networks projected Joe Biden as the winner, Trump and his allies flooded the media with unsubstantiated claims, ranging from dead people voting to baseless accusations that voting machines were rigged. These claims fueled protests, triggered violent threats against election officials, and ultimately culminated in the January 6 Capitol insurrection.

Despite the volume of fraud allegations, no credible evidence has ever supported the claim that the 2020 election was stolen. Independent audits, bipartisan recounts, and court rulings—including decisions from Republican-appointed judges—have consistently confirmed the election was fair and that Biden legitimately won. Even officials from Trump's administration, including Attorney General William Barr and senior figures in the Department of Homeland Security, publicly refuted the fraud claims.

However, the persistence of the "stolen election" narrative reveals the power of misinformation, the effectiveness of repetition in political propaganda, and the role of partisan media in shaping public perception. This manufactured doubt in the electoral process has had wide-reaching consequences: justifying restrictive voting laws, undermining faith in democratic institutions, and radicalizing segments of the electorate against the very systems that uphold free and fair elections.

Context:

1. Court Rulings and Investigations

Trump and his legal team aggressively challenged the election results, filing over 60 lawsuits in battleground states such as Georgia, Pennsylvania, Michigan, and Arizona. Judges—many of them appointed by Republicans, including Trump himself—dismissed the vast majority of these cases due to a complete lack of evidence. Courts repeatedly found the claims legally baseless and factually unsupported. In one ruling, a Pennsylvania judge wrote that the Trump campaign presented "strained legal arguments without merit and speculative accusations" (Trump v. Boockvar, 2020).

Even Trump's Justice Department, led by Attorney General Barr, found no evidence to support the fraud claims. In December 2020, Barr publicly stated that the DOJ had uncovered no fraud on a scale that could have altered the election outcome. State election officials from both parties confirmed the integrity of the results. Recounts—including a Republican-led audit in Arizona's Maricopa County—reaffirmed Biden's victory.

Despite these definitive findings, Trump and his allies refused to accept the outcome. They doubled down on false claims, continuing to spread disinformation that eroded public trust in the electoral system. This campaign of deceit fueled calls for unnecessary voting restrictions and hardened partisan divides.

Polls consistently show that a majority of Republican voters still believe the election was fraudulent, despite the overwhelming evidence to the contrary. This demonstrates the challenge of countering misinformation once it becomes embedded in political identity. For many Trump supporters, belief in a "stolen election" has moved beyond facts; it now functions as an emotional and ideological anchor that reinforces distrust in institutions and unwavering loyalty to Trump.

2. The Role of Conspiracy Theories

The myth of the stolen election was not merely a political talking point—it was a conspiracy theory deliberately cultivated and amplified across right-wing media. One of the most damaging claims was that voting machines, particularly those made by Dominion Voting Systems, had been rigged to flip Trump votes to Biden. Promoted by figures like Rudy Giuliani, Sidney Powell, and MyPillow CEO Mike Lindell, these accusations gained traction despite being repeatedly debunked by election officials and independent fact-checkers. The spread of these falsehoods was no accident; it was part of a calculated strategy to keep Trump's base engaged, enraged, and mobilized.

Conservative networks such as Fox News, One America News Network (OANN), and Newsmax gave these conspiracy theories a national platform, lending them credibility among millions of viewers. This helped erode trust in the electoral process, sparked threats against election workers, and fueled a movement demanding endless "audits" long after results had been certified. These lies, however, came with consequences. Dominion Voting Systems filed multi-billion-dollar defamation lawsuits against the media outlets and individuals who knowingly spread false claims. In April 2023, Fox News settled with Dominion for $787 million—a tacit admission that it had broadcast lies about election fraud to appease its audience.

Even as court rulings and legal penalties mounted, the election fraud narrative remained central to Trump's political identity. For his base, it evolved into more than a belief about 2020—it became an article of faith used to justify restrictive voting laws, opposition to democratic norms, and even violent insurrection. The persistence of the "Big Lie" reveals how vulnerable democratic institutions become when allegiance to a political figure outweighs commitment to objective truth.

This disinformation campaign did not fade after the election; it continues to shape Republican policy and rhetoric. Legislatures in GOP-controlled states have used the false narrative of widespread voter fraud to justify new voting restrictions, including stricter voter ID laws, limits on mail-in voting, and increased partisan control over election administration. Trump and his allies have also worked to install election deniers in key positions of power, raising the risk that future elections may be more vulnerable to partisan interference than in 2020.

The "Big Lie" is not just about Trump's refusal to concede—it represents a broader assault on democracy. It has created a dangerous precedent where losing candidates can claim fraud without evidence, paving the way for future challenges to legitimate election outcomes. By undermining faith in the electoral system, the MAGA movement has fostered an environment where political violence, voter suppression, and election subversion pose real threats to democratic governance. Recognizing the role of misinformation in this movement is essential to safeguarding democracy from future attacks on its legitimacy.

Claim: "The Media Is Covering Up the Fraud"

Trump and his allies have repeatedly alleged that mainstream media outlets actively concealed evidence of election fraud, portraying journalists as part of a vast conspiracy to protect Biden's victory. This narrative claims that major outlets such as CNN, The New York Times, and The Washington Post not only failed to investigate fraud allegations but also deliberately suppressed key information that could have exposed the so-called "stolen election."

This accusation served two purposes: it discredited any reporting contradicting Trump's narrative and reinforced the belief that only MAGA-aligned sources could be trusted. By attacking the credibility of mainstream news, Trump positioned himself as the sole source of truth for his followers, further insulating them from factual reporting that refuted the fraud claims.

This tactic mirrors authoritarian leaders' strategies to delegitimize independent journalism and maintain control over public perception. The claim of a media "cover-up" was never about uncovering actual evidence—it was about controlling the narrative and ensuring that Trump's base remained distrustful of any information that challenged their beliefs.

Context:

1. Media Responsibility and Fact-Checking

Far from covering up fraud, mainstream media outlets played a critical role in debunking the baseless claims surrounding the 2020 election. Investigative journalists and independent fact-checkers thoroughly examined allegations of voter fraud, publishing in-depth analyses that exposed misinformation and falsehoods. Organizations like PolitiFact, The Washington Post's Fact Checker, and FactCheck.org systematically dismantled claims about rigged voting machines, deceased individuals casting ballots, and large-scale dumps of fraudulent votes. Their reporting was grounded in official data, sworn testimony, and court rulings—all of which confirmed the security of the 2020 election.

Major news outlets also extensively covered the legal battles that followed the election, including the more than 60 court cases filed by Trump's legal team, many of which were dismissed due to a lack of evidence. Additionally, they reported on audits and recounts, such as the aforementioned Republican-led review in Arizona's Maricopa County, which only reaffirmed Biden's victory.

Despite these facts, right-wing media personalities and MAGA influencers aggressively pushed the narrative that these fact-checking efforts were not legitimate journalism but part of a coordinated "deep state" plot to suppress the truth. This false claim proved incredibly persuasive among Trump's base, reinforcing existing distrust of mainstream media and encouraging greater reliance on conservative-aligned outlets like Fox News, OANN, and Newsmax—platforms that actively promoted election fraud conspiracies. By labeling all contradictory information as "fake news," Trump and his allies fostered an environment in which objective facts became irrelevant to many of his supporters.

2. The Consequences of Media Distrust

The claim that the media covered up election fraud significantly contributed to the erosion of public trust in democratic institutions. By convincing millions of Americans that mainstream journalism was dishonest and corrupt, Trump and his allies undermined faith in the electoral system itself. The consequences have been lasting: a substantial portion of Republican voters still believe the election was stolen, despite overwhelming evidence to the contrary. This manufactured distrust in both the press and democratic processes has fueled support for extreme measures—including state-level election interference, restrictive voting laws, and even political violence.

One of the most serious consequences of this distrust was the January 6th attack on the U.S. Capitol. Many of the rioters explicitly cited their belief that the election had been stolen and that the media were lying about it. The willingness of Trump's supporters to reject all mainstream reporting in favor of right-wing propaganda created an environment in which misinformation translated directly into real-world violence.

The "media cover-up" narrative was not solely about election fraud—it was part of a broader strategy to delegitimize any authority that contradicted Trump's version of events. By positioning himself as the only trustworthy figure, Trump ensured that his followers would reject inconvenient facts as "fake news," creating a feedback loop in which misinformation thrived unchecked. This dynamic remains a defining feature of the MAGA movement and poses one of the most significant ongoing challenges to restoring trust in democratic institutions and independent journalism.

3. The Consequences of the Big Lie

The most dangerous consequence of the Big Lie was the January 6th insurrection at the U.S. Capitol. Convinced they were defending democracy, a mob of Trump supporters stormed the Capitol to prevent Congress from certifying Joe Biden's victory. This attack, which resulted in deaths, assaults on law enforcement, and a temporary halt to the constitutional process, was a direct outcome of Trump's relentless election fraud claims. His refusal to accept defeat and repeated calls to "stop the steal" created a sense of urgency and desperation among his base, laying the groundwork for violent action.

On the morning of January 6th, Trump addressed his supporters at the "Save America" rally, urging them to march to the Capitol and "fight like hell" or risk losing their country. Although he briefly mentioned protesting "peacefully and patriotically," the overall tone of his speech was one of defiance, reinforcing the false claim that the election had been stolen. His rhetoric, along with inflammatory statements from allies like Rudy Giuliani and Rep. Mo Brooks, escalated tensions and gave rioters a sense of mission. Many later testified that they believed they were following Trump's orders as they stormed the Capitol, chanting threats against lawmakers and violently clashing with police.

As the attack unfolded, Trump failed to act swiftly to stop the violence. Reports indicate he watched the chaos unfold on television, expressing approval of the crowd's size while ignoring pleas from advisors and lawmakers to intervene. When he finally addressed his supporters, he issued a weak call for peace but reiterated his false claims, telling the rioters, "We love you. You are exceptional." His delayed and dismissive response underscored his role in inciting the attack and continued prioritizing personal power over democratic stability.

The insurrection was not an isolated event—it was the culmination of months of lies, conspiracy theories, and deliberate incitement. It exposed the fragility of American democracy and demonstrated the real-world consequences of political misinformation. Even after the violence, Trump and his allies continued to promote the Big Lie, fueling ongoing threats to the electoral system, justifying restrictive voting laws, and ensuring future elections remain vulnerable to baseless challenges. January 6th was not just an attack on the Capitol—it was an attack on democracy itself, revealing the dangers of a movement that values loyalty to a leader over objective reality.

4. The Incitement of Violence

Trump's refusal to accept the results of the election and his continued promotion of baseless fraud claims directly contributed to the violence on January 6th. In the months following the election, he held rallies and repeatedly pushed the idea that the election had been stolen. This culminated in his speech on the morning of the Capitol attack, where he encouraged supporters to "peacefully and patriotically" protest—but also to "fight like hell" (Trump, 2021). His words, paired with months of inflammatory rhetoric, helped create the conditions for a violent uprising.

The insurrection was not a spontaneous outburst—it was the culmination of a disinformation campaign that had been building since Election Day. The FBI and other law enforcement agencies later confirmed that many of the individuals involved were motivated by the false belief that the election was stolen. This underscores both the fragility of American democracy and the power of misinformation to incite real-world violence.

Moreover, the attack on the Capitol revealed that many within Trump's base were willing to abandon democratic norms in favor of political violence. Some rioters openly called for the execution of elected officials, including then-Vice President Mike Pence. This unprecedented assault on the legislative branch was not just an attack on a building—it was an attack on the peaceful transfer of power, a foundational principle of American democracy.

The Ongoing Impact on American Democracy

The continued belief in the Big Lie remains a growing threat to democracy in the U.S. According to polling, more than half of Republicans still believe the 2020 election was stolen, despite overwhelming evidence to the contrary (Ipsos, 2021). This widespread acceptance of false claims not only undermines trust in the electoral process but has also reshaped the Republican Party itself. Embracing the Big Lie has become a de facto loyalty test—rejecting Trump's falsehoods can lead to political exile. Republican officials who acknowledged Biden's legitimate victory, such as Liz Cheney and Adam Kinzinger, have faced primary defeats, party censure, or removal from leadership roles.

Voter fraud is minuscule in U.S. elections
Share of reported cases of fraud over the past 13 to 38 years is less than 1%

State	Heritage Foundation number of years analyzed	Number of elections held*	Total ballots (for reporting years)	Number of reported cases of fraud	Percent fraudulent votes
Arizona	25	36	42,626,379	36	**0.0000845%**
Georgia	27	34	64,742,598	23	**0.0000355%**
Michigan	17 (first case in 2007 about 2005 election)	26	64,520,604	19	**0.0000294%**
Nevada	13	14	8,506,824	8	**0.0000940%**
North Carolina	38	39	81,677,000	58	**0.0000710%**
Pennsylvania	30	32	100,526,098	39	**0.0000388%**
Wisconsin	20	28	45,329,695	69	**0.0001522%**

Source: Heritage Foundation Voter Fraud Database

Note: *Elections counted include midterms, presidential, and special elections.

B Governance Studies at BROOKINGS

The effects of the Big Lie extend well beyond public opinion—they have fueled legislative efforts that threaten voting rights. Republican-controlled states have passed restrictive voting laws under the pretext of "election security," despite no evidence of widespread fraud. These laws disproportionately affect Black and Latino voters, exacerbating existing racial inequalities in the political system (Brennan Center for Justice, 2021). Though justified by misinformation, these laws are actively reshaping the voting landscape in ways that could suppress participation in future elections.

Moreover, the false election fraud narrative has emboldened anti-democratic forces within the GOP. Trump and his allies have worked to install election-denying candidates in influential positions, including secretaries of state and local election boards. If such individuals refuse to certify legitimate election results, the country could face a more severe constitutional crisis than the one in 2020.

The Big Lie has not only fueled political violence but also set a dangerous precedent for the future of U.S. elections. If a large portion of the public believes elections are routinely stolen, the legitimacy of future outcomes will be questioned, making peaceful transitions of power increasingly tricky. This ongoing attack on democracy will persist unless the influence of the Big Lie is confronted with truth and accountability. Without action, the foundation of the American electoral system will remain at serious risk.

The persistence of the Big Lie is not just about one election—it represents a broader challenge to the very idea of objective truth in American politics. By rejecting evidence and embracing conspiracy theories, the MAGA movement has demonstrated a willingness to undermine democracy in pursuit of power. This disinformation campaign has fundamentally reshaped the Republican Party, making election denialism a core part of its platform. Confronting and countering this threat is essential to preserving the resilience of American democracy in the years ahead.

Key takeaways

- The claim that the 2020 election was stolen from Trump is baseless and repeatedly debunked by courts, audits, and even Trump's own officials.

- The "Big Lie" became central to MAGA identity, fueling distrust in democracy and inciting the January 6th Capitol insurrection.

- Right-wing media played a crucial role in spreading conspiracy theories, leading to billion-dollar lawsuits and long-term damage to public trust.

- The narrative of election fraud has driven restrictive voting laws and empowered election deniers, threatening future democratic processes.

- Media discrediting and conspiracy rhetoric have created an echo chamber where facts are dismissed, and loyalty to Trump outweighs truth.

Chapter Twelve
Foreign Policy

The Myth of Trump's "Peace Presidency"

Donald Trump and his supporters often repeat the phrase "no new wars," portraying his presidency as a model of non-interventionist foreign policy. Trump frequently boasted that, unlike his predecessors, he avoided costly military entanglements and prioritized diplomacy over conflict. This narrative has become central to the MAGA movement's depiction of Trump as a leader who put "America First" while keeping the country out of foreign wars.

However, this simplified framing overlooks the realities of Trump's foreign policy, which was frequently erratic, marked by escalations, and shaped by unpredictable decision-making. While he did not initiate a large-scale war, his administration engaged in significant military actions, withdrew from critical diplomatic agreements, and heightened tensions with key adversaries—often bringing the U.S. to the brink of conflict. Trump's rhetoric on peace often clashed with his administration's aggressive posturing, and his approach to diplomacy frequently undermined long-term global stability.

Claim: "Trump Started No New Wars"

Trump and his supporters frequently cite his presidency as one of military restraint, contrasting it with George W. Bush and Barack Obama. He positioned himself as a leader determined to end "endless wars," often highlighting his efforts to withdraw troops and reduce U.S. involvement in foreign conflicts.

While it is technically accurate that Trump did not formally declare a new war, this claim obscures a more complex reality. His foreign policy decisions often escalated global tensions and increased military engagements in various regions. Far from being a consistent peace advocate, Trump's actions abroad reflected a pattern of unpredictability and confrontation that, at times, pushed the United States closer to open conflict.

Context:

1. The Absence of New Large-Scale Wars

Trump's claim that he did not start any new wars is technically accurate, but it overlooks the broader implications of his foreign policy decisions. Unlike George W. Bush, who launched full-scale invasions of Iraq and Afghanistan, or Barack Obama, who led NATO's intervention in Libya, Trump did not initiate a comparable large-scale military campaign. He used this fact to portray himself as fundamentally different from his predecessors, branding himself a disruptor who rejected past interventionist policies. His "America First" agenda—emphasizing withdrawal from foreign conflicts and a renewed focus on domestic priorities—resonated with many Americans disillusioned by decades of costly military entanglements.

However, a closer examination of Trump's military and foreign policy record reveals a pattern that complicates the notion of his administration as truly non-interventionist.

Rather than committing to a consistent strategy of reducing U.S. military involvement, Trump often made abrupt, politically motivated decisions that disrupted ongoing operations without fully disengaging from conflict zones. His 2019 withdrawal of U.S. forces from northern Syria is a key example. The announcement came with little warning to military officials or allies, leaving Kurdish forces, key U.S. partners in the fight against ISIS, exposed. This decision cleared the way for a Turkish offensive, resulting in civilian casualties, mass displacement, and a resurgence of ISIS activity. While Trump framed the move as fulfilling a promise to bring troops home, critics argued that it abandoned key allies and created a power vacuum swiftly exploited by adversaries.

Similarly, Trump's troop drawdown in Afghanistan was driven more by campaign optics than a cohesive long-term strategy. His administration negotiated a deal with the Taliban that laid the groundwork for a complete U.S. withdrawal. However, the agreement was widely criticized as one-sided and lacking meaningful concessions from the Taliban. By enabling the Taliban's resurgence without securing protections for the Afghan government, Trump's deal set the stage for the country's collapse after his presidency. Though troop levels fell, American involvement in the conflict remained, and regional instability grew.

While Trump frequently boasted about bringing troops home, his administration also deployed additional forces in response to escalating tensions. After the 2020 assassination of Iranian General Qasem

Soleimani, the U.S. sent thousands of troops to the Middle East amid fears of a broader conflict with Iran. Similarly, Trump increased military support to Saudi Arabia during its war in Yemen—a conflict that contributed to one of the world's worst humanitarian crises. These actions illustrate that although he avoided initiating new wars, Trump was willing to escalate military engagement when it suited his strategic or political goals.

Trump's approach to foreign policy is best described as selective interventionism rather than genuine restraint. He avoided large-scale invasions but embraced tactical military escalations that heightened global instability, deepened reliance on proxy conflicts, and allowed adversaries to strengthen their positions. Rather than representing a clean break from interventionism, his foreign policy marked a shift in tactics that often produced chaotic and unintended consequences.

2. The Escalation of Drone Strikes and Military Operations

A defining feature of Trump's foreign policy was the sharp expansion of drone warfare. Under his administration, the United States increased drone strikes in conflict zones such as Yemen, Somalia, and Pakistan, significantly surpassing the number carried out under his predecessors. While drone warfare had been a core part of U.S. counterterrorism strategy since the Bush and Obama administrations, Trump's approach removed many existing restrictions and oversight mechanisms, allowing for more strikes with fewer bureaucratic delays.

One major shift came in 2017 when Trump rolled back Obama-era policies requiring high-level White House approval for drone strikes outside active war zones. This change gave the Pentagon and CIA greater autonomy in conducting drone operations, leading to a sharp increase in airstrikes, particularly in regions where the U.S. maintained a counterterrorism presence without being formally at war. In Somalia, for example, the U.S. military carried out at least 200 drone strikes between 2017 and 2021, compared to fewer than 50 during Obama's second term (The Bureau of Investigative Journalism, 2021). In Yemen, drone strikes more than doubled under Trump, and although operations in Pakistan declined from their peak under Obama, they continued as part of broader counterterrorism efforts.

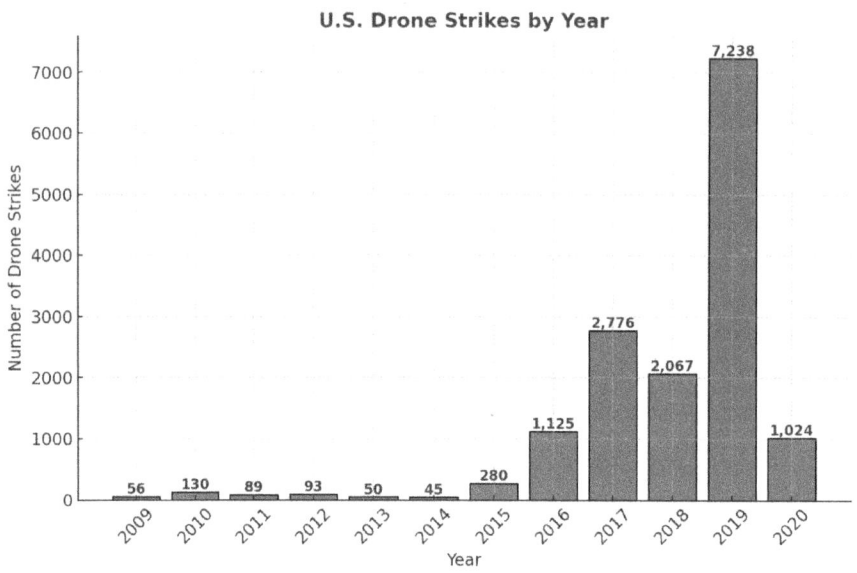

Trump and his supporters framed this approach as a more efficient way to eliminate terrorist threats, but the reality was more complex. Civilian casualties remained a persistent concern, with estimates suggesting that hundreds of non-combatants were killed during Trump's presidency (Airwars, 2021). Drone strikes, often based on incomplete or flawed intelligence, frequently resulted in mistaken identities and unintended deaths. Without on-the-ground verification, many reported "militant"

deaths may have included civilians misidentified as threats. The secrecy surrounding drone operations also made it challenging to hold military and intelligence agencies accountable for errors.

The long-term consequences of Trump's expanded drone program fueled resentment toward the U.S. in affected regions. Civilian deaths and the perception of unchecked American force created fertile ground for extremist recruitment. Groups like al-Qaeda and ISIS exploited the anger generated by these strikes to attract new members, using them as evidence of Western aggression against Muslim nations. Although some high-value targets were eliminated, the broader impact of escalated drone warfare may have been counterproductive, further destabilizing already fragile states and deepening anti-American sentiment.

Beyond conventional drone warfare, Trump's foreign policy also featured high-profile targeted assassinations, most notably the January 2020 killing of Iranian General Qasem Soleimani. As commander of Iran's Quds Force, Soleimani was a key architect of Iran's regional military strategy, supporting proxy groups in Syria, Iraq, Lebanon, and Yemen. The drone strike that killed him near Baghdad International Airport was unprecedented in targeting a senior military official of a sovereign nation.

The Trump administration justified the assassination as a counterterrorism measure, arguing that Soleimani was responsible for attacks on U.S. personnel and was planning further assaults. However, the repercussions were immediate and significant. In retaliation, Iran launched missile strikes on U.S. bases in Iraq, injuring more than 100 American troops. Although the situation did not escalate into full-scale war, the killing brought U.S.-Iran relations to the brink of open conflict. It also set a troubling precedent, suggesting the U.S. was willing to carry out extrajudicial killings of foreign officials—an action condemned by Iran and criticized by several U.S. allies, who feared such tactics could provoke further instability.

Trump's decision to authorize the Soleimani strike without consulting Congress also reignited debates over executive war powers. Critics argued that he had sidestepped the War Powers Resolution, which requires congressional approval for military actions that could lead to sustained conflict. While the administration claimed national security justified the strike, many saw it as an unnecessary provocation that could have quickly spiraled into a broader regional war.

3. The Withdrawal from the Iran Nuclear Deal

Trump's unilateral withdrawal from the Iran nuclear deal—formally known as the Joint Comprehensive Plan of Action (JCPOA)—significantly reshaped U.S. foreign policy in the Middle East, complicating efforts to manage Iran's nuclear ambitions and regional influence. The agreement, brokered under the Obama administration, was designed to limit Iran's ability to develop nuclear weapons in exchange for lifting economic sanctions. By pulling out of the deal in 2018 and reimposing severe sanctions, Trump dismantled a key diplomatic achievement that had successfully curbed Iran's nuclear program and fostered international cooperation. His decision, based on the belief that the JCPOA was too lenient and failed to address Iran's ballistic missile program and regional proxy activities, created immediate instability. Iran, which had largely complied with the deal, responded by resuming uranium enrichment beyond the agreed-upon limits, heightening fears of a nuclear-armed Iran.

The decision reignited tensions between the U.S. and Iran and strained relations with key American allies, particularly those in Europe who had helped craft the JCPOA. France, Germany, and the United Kingdom condemned the move, arguing that abandoning the deal weakened diplomatic credibility and made future negotiations more difficult. By dismissing the concerns of longstanding partners, Trump reinforced the perception that the U.S. was willing to act unilaterally, even at the cost of traditional alliances. Moreover, the withdrawal justified Iran to expand its nuclear activities, further destabilizing the region and increasing the risk of conflict.

The withdrawal had broader geopolitical consequences beyond the immediate effects on Iran's nuclear program. The reimposition of harsh sanctions under Trump's "maximum pressure" campaign devastated Iran's economy but failed to produce the regime change or diplomatic concessions he had anticipated. Instead, Iran responded with escalatory actions: attacking oil tankers in the Persian Gulf, shooting down a U.S. drone, and launching missile strikes on U.S. bases in Iraq. These events pushed the U.S. and Iran closer to direct military confrontation, undermining Trump's claim that his foreign policy promoted peace and de-escalation. The JCPOA withdrawal—combined with the 2020 assassination of Iranian General Qasem Soleimani—cemented a pattern of provocation over diplomacy, escalating tensions, and making conflict more likely.

In short, while Trump did not start a full-scale war with Iran, his foreign policy choices significantly increased the risk of one. Exiting the JCPOA reversed years of diplomatic progress and contributed to a more volatile, unpredictable geopolitical environment. The consequences—accelerated Iranian nuclear development and broader regional instability—illustrate how his actions often undermined, rather than strengthened, U.S. security interests. The portrayal of Trump as a "peace president" ignores these realities. His decisions frequently fueled tensions and set the stage for future conflicts instead of preventing them.

Claim: "Trump Was Tough on China"

A central pillar of Trump's foreign policy was his stance on China, which he repeatedly labeled a strategic competitor and economic threat. His administration's actions—including launching a trade war, imposing tariffs, and accusing China of intellectual property theft—positioned Beijing as a key adversary on the global stage. Trump's confrontational approach resonated with many supporters, especially those who believed China's rise was undermining American manufacturing and displacing U.S. workers. However, despite his rhetoric, the actual effectiveness of his China policy remains widely debated.

Context:

1. Economic Impact on American Consumers and Businesses

Trump's trade war with China—launched to address trade imbalances, curb intellectual property theft, and reshore jobs—resulted in significant economic repercussions for American consumers and businesses. Imposing tariffs on Chinese goods increased costs across multiple sectors, functioning more as an economic burden than a driver of anticipated benefits. These tariffs made a wide range of consumer products more expensive, from electronics to household essentials, placing added financial strain on American households and prompting changes in spending behavior. Research shows that many households reduced spending on services while accelerating the purchase of goods to avoid further anticipated price hikes (Investopedia, n.d.). This shift directly responded to the inflationary pressures introduced by the trade policies.

The tariffs meant higher operational costs for businesses, especially those reliant on Chinese manufacturing. Companies were faced with either absorbing these expenses, which cut into profit margins, or passing them on to consumers, potentially diminishing their competitiveness. Industries such as manufacturing and agriculture, which had deeply integrated supply chains with China, were significantly affected. Many businesses were forced to reevaluate their supply chains, often incurring substantial costs to shift to alternative suppliers or production hubs.

American farmers were among those hit hardest. China imposed retaliatory tariffs on U.S. agricultural exports, targeting key commodities like soybeans, pork, and corn in response to U.S. tariffs. This led to a sharp drop in export revenues. Between 2018 and 2019, U.S. agricultural exports declined by more than $27 billion, with China accounting for approximately 95% of that loss (U.S. Department of Agriculture [USDA], 2021). The federal government introduced subsidies totaling tens of billions of dollars to offset the damage. However, these payments were funded by American taxpayers, effectively transferring the economic burden of the trade war onto the domestic population.

The trade war's impact went beyond immediate financial losses. Uncertainty surrounding tariff enforcement and the threat of additional retaliatory measures fueled market volatility and deterred business investment. Some analysts warned of the risk of recession. For example, Goldman Sachs estimated a 35% chance of a U.S. recession within the year, citing policy uncertainty and rising inflation as key concerns (New York Magazine, 2019). Moreover, the trade war failed to deliver its core objectives. The U.S. trade deficit with China remained significant, and concerns like intellectual property theft and forced technology transfers persisted. Rather than forcing China to change its trade practices, the tariffs prolonged economic tensions without yielding meaningful reform.

In short, while the trade war was framed as a strategy to strengthen the U.S. economy and confront unfair trade practices, it ultimately raised consumer costs, inflicted losses on businesses, especially in agriculture, and introduced more significant economic uncertainty. The promised outcomes of reshoring jobs and reducing trade imbalances largely failed to materialize, leaving American industries and consumers to shoulder the costs of these policies.

2. Disruption to Global Supply Chains

Trump's tariffs disrupted trade between the U.S. and China and had far-reaching effects on global supply chains, which had been optimized over decades of economic globalization. The uncertainty caused by fluctuating tariff rates, abrupt policy shifts, and retaliatory measures forced companies across multiple industries to reassess their production strategies. Businesses that relied on Chinese manufacturers for components, particularly in the electronics, automotive, and consumer goods sectors, were left with two choices: absorb higher costs or shift production to other countries.

This realignment was neither immediate nor inexpensive. Relocating supply chains required substantial investments in infrastructure, workforce training, and regulatory compliance in new markets. Some firms moved operations to Southeast Asian countries such as Vietnam, Thailand, and Malaysia to avoid tariffs. However, these nations often lacked China's industrial scale and efficiency, resulting in additional delays and inefficiencies (Bown, 2020). Rather than incentivizing a broad return of manufacturing to the U.S., the tariffs largely redirected production to other low-cost regions, underscoring the complexities of global trade interdependence.

Beyond the tariff war, other structural factors compounded supply chain disruptions. Although COVID-19 is often cited as a major contributor to supply chain instability, several non-pandemic-related issues also played a role. Rising labor costs in China—driven by wage growth and the country's transition to a more high-tech economy—had already encouraged companies to diversify their manufacturing bases even before the trade war began. In addition, environmental regulations and energy constraints within China affected production capacity, particularly in highly polluting industries like steel, textiles, and electronics (Daly, 2019).

Geopolitical tensions beyond the U.S.-China relationship added to the strain. Brexit introduced logistical uncertainty for companies operating between the U.K. and the European Union, complicating cross-border trade and delaying the movement of goods. Simultaneously, increased cyberattacks on critical infrastructure, such as ransomware assaults on significant logistics firms, further exposed vulnerabilities in global supply networks (Lee, 2021).

Trump's trade policies did not operate in a vacuum. They amplified global supply chains' challenges, including rising costs, evolving regulations, and geopolitical instability. Instead of facilitating a controlled decoupling from China in a way that benefited American industry, the tariffs triggered costly disruptions without addressing deeper structural dependencies. The resulting instability left businesses scrambling to adapt, driving up costs for producers and consumers, while failing to spark a manufacturing revival in the United States.

3. Unresolved Structural Issues with China

Although the trade war was framed as a necessary confrontation to force China into fairer economic practices, it failed to address the deeply rooted structural differences between the two economies. China's economic model relies heavily on state intervention, industrial subsidies, and strategic planning to dominate key industries. The tariffs did little to curb these practices. China continued supporting state-owned enterprises and investing in high-tech sectors like artificial intelligence, 5G, and semiconductor production. Rather than compelling reform, the trade war may have strengthened Beijing's resolve to reduce reliance on the U.S. by accelerating domestic innovation and forging new trade partnerships (Lardy, 2020).

Intellectual property theft and forced technology transfers—two major grievances cited by the Trump administration—remained persistent throughout the trade war. The Phase One trade deal included vague commitments from China to strengthen intellectual property protections, but enforcement mechanisms were weak (Bown, 2020). China's long-term strategy of acquiring foreign technology—legally and illicitly—persisted, and American companies continued facing pressure to share proprietary information for market access. This exposed the limitations of tariffs as a tool to compel reform in a system where state intervention is deeply entrenched.

Despite Trump's harsh rhetoric, the U.S.-China trade deficit did not meaningfully or sustainably decline. While tariffs briefly reduced imports from China, American firms turned to other low-cost manufacturing hubs rather than reshoring production to the U.S. Instead of reducing foreign dependency, the trade war primarily led to supply chain shifts to countries like Vietnam and India (Daly, 2019). This highlighted a key flaw in Trump's approach—tariffs were a blunt instrument ill-suited to addressing the complex challenges of globalization, automation, and industrial competitiveness.

Meanwhile, China's global influence continued to grow despite U.S. tariffs. Though bilateral trade was disrupted, Beijing advanced its broader economic ambitions through initiatives like the Belt and Road Initiative (BRI), deepening ties with countries in Africa, Latin America, and Europe. These partnerships lessened the impact of U.S. trade restrictions and secured China's access to critical markets and resources. Concurrently, China solidified its position as a global leader in manufacturing and technological innovation, remaining central to the global economy despite U.S. efforts to isolate it (Lee, 2021).

While Trump's tariffs signaled a hardline stance on China, they failed to shift the balance of economic power between the two nations. Rather than forcing concessions, the trade war revealed the limits of unilateral economic pressure in a world defined by interconnected supply chains, financial markets, and technological ecosystems. The absence of a coherent, long-term strategy meant that the trade war produced short-term disruptions without resolving the deeper structural issues that define U.S.-China economic relations. Without a comprehensive plan that includes multilateral diplomacy, strategic investment in U.S. industries, and strengthened international trade alliances, future efforts to counter China's economic practices risk repeating the same mistakes.

Claim: " Trump Strengthened America's Global Standing"

Trump and his allies have portrayed his "America First" policies as a bold reassertion of U.S. strength and dominance in international affairs. Supporters argue that his confrontational approach to trade, defense, and diplomacy restored American leverage and forced allies and adversaries alike to respect U.S. interests. However, rather than solidifying global leadership, Trump's policies frequently alienated allies, eroded diplomatic trust and diminished America's influence in key international institutions. His withdrawal from multilateral agreements, trade wars, and unpredictable foreign policy decisions often left the U.S. isolated, allowing strategic rivals like China and Russia to expand their global influence while traditional allies questioned America's reliability.

Context:

1. Isolation Under Trump

While Trump's rhetoric claimed to restore American strength, his actions often left the U.S. more isolated globally. His retreat from multilateral engagement created a leadership vacuum that strategic competitors—particularly China and Russia—quickly exploited. By withdrawing from key international agreements and reducing U.S. participation in global institutions, Trump opened the door for China to expand its economic and diplomatic influence through initiatives like the Belt and Road Initiative (BRI). As the U.S. withdrew from partnerships in the Pacific, China deepened its economic ties across Asia, Africa, and Latin America, positioning itself as the dominant global trading partner in regions where the U.S. had traditionally held influence. America's absence allowed Beijing to shape the terms of economic cooperation, secure critical infrastructure contracts, and expand its role in global governance.

Russia also capitalized on the fractures within Western alliances, particularly NATO, which Trump repeatedly criticized and undermined. His contradictory messaging—questioning the alliance's relevance while demanding higher financial contributions—sowed doubt among European allies and emboldened Moscow's assertive foreign policy. Russia expanded its influence in Eastern Europe, the Middle East, and Africa, weakening the perception of the U.S. as a reliable partner.

The long-term consequences of diminished American leadership extended beyond traditional geopolitics. Institutions like the United Nations, World Trade Organization, and G7 increasingly operated without clear U.S. leadership, as the country prioritized nationalist policies over cooperative problem-solving. This shift weakened America's ability to shape global norms and reduced its diplomatic leverage in addressing cybersecurity, arms control, and international trade. Although Trump framed his "America First" approach as a display of strength, it often produced the opposite effect, generating uncertainty, straining alliances, and empowering strategic rivals.

2. The Afghanistan Withdrawal – A Chaotic Legacy

One of the most consequential and controversial foreign policy decisions of Trump's presidency was his agreement with the Taliban to withdraw U.S. troops from Afghanistan. In February 2020, the Trump administration signed the Doha Agreement, setting a timeline for a complete American withdrawal in exchange for vague Taliban commitments to curb terrorist activity and engage in peace talks with the Afghan government. Trump framed the deal as a fulfillment of his promise to end America's involvement in the "forever wars," arguing that continued military engagement was no longer in the national interest.

However, the agreement lacked strict enforcement mechanisms, did not require the Taliban to halt attacks on Afghan security forces, and offered little accountability. By negotiating directly with the Taliban and sidelining the Afghan government, Trump's administration weakened Kabul's legitimacy. It emboldened insurgents who saw the withdrawal as an impending victory rather than a diplomatic compromise.

The rapid collapse of the Afghan government and the Taliban's swift return to power in 2021 exposed the weaknesses of this strategy. Although the withdrawal was carried out under the Biden administration, Trump's agreement laid the groundwork for the chaotic and disastrous evacuation. The absence of clear contingencies in the Doha Agreement, combined with Trump's decision to begin reducing troop levels before conditions were met, created a power vacuum that hastened the fall of Afghanistan's democratic government. The resulting humanitarian crisis, including images of desperate Afghans clinging to departing U.S. aircraft, cast serious doubt on Trump's claims of projecting strength and stability. Instead, it reinforced the perception that the U.S. was willing to abandon its allies, undermining American credibility on the world stage.

Trump frequently positioned himself as a "peace president" who avoided new wars, but his foreign policy record paints a different picture. While he did not initiate large-scale military interventions, several of his actions escalated global tensions. The targeted killing of Iranian General Qasem Soleimani in early 2020 brought the U.S. to the brink of war with Iran, prompting retaliatory missile strikes on U.S. bases in Iraq. Trump's

2018 withdrawal from the Iran nuclear deal increased the risk of Iran pursuing nuclear weapons, heightening instability in the region. Similarly, his trade war with China failed to resolve major economic disputes and disrupted global supply chains, contributing to economic uncertainty.

China, in particular, capitalized on the U.S.'s retreat from global leadership. As America disengaged from multilateral agreements and international institutions, China expanded its influence through initiatives like the Belt and Road Initiative, deepening its economic and diplomatic ties across Africa, Latin America, and Asia. While Trump withdrew the U.S. from global pacts, China positioned itself as a trade, infrastructure, and climate diplomacy leader. In Afghanistan, the U.S. withdrawal created a strategic opening for China, which quickly engaged with the Taliban to pursue economic deals and secure access to the country's mineral resources.

Ultimately, Trump's retreat from global leadership facilitated China's rise and undercut America's international standing. Far from reinforcing U.S. dominance, his policies often left the country isolated and empowered adversaries to expand their influence at America's expense.

Key takeaways

- Trump didn't start a new large-scale war, but he escalated tensions with Iran, withdrew from key agreements, and destabilized regions like Syria.

- His foreign policy was marked by erratic decision-making, such as the Soleimani assassination and withdrawal from the Iran nuclear deal.

- Drone strikes increased dramatically under Trump, with reduced oversight and a rise in civilian casualties.

- The trade war with China hurt American consumers and farmers while failing to bring meaningful reforms or reduce the trade deficit.

- Trump's "America First" approach isolated the U.S. internationally, weakened alliances, and empowered adversaries like China and Russia.

PART 04

RECLAIMING THE NARRATIVE— HOW DEMOCRATS CAN WIN IN A MAGA WORLD

Chapter Thirteen
A Better Vision for America

The rise of the MAGA movement has deepened divisions in American politics, with fear, misinformation, and identity politics often dominating the national conversation. Identity politics refers to political strategies and discourse that center on the experiences and interests of specific social groups, such as those based on race, gender, or sexual orientation. While addressing systemic inequality is essential, a narrowly framed focus on identity-based appeals can sometimes alienate voters who feel that cultural debates are overshadowing their economic concerns.

To reclaim the political narrative, Democrats need more than just a rebuttal to MAGA's falsehoods—they must articulate a compelling vision that speaks to the needs of all Americans, especially those who feel excluded from the current political dialogue. To truly connect with working-class voters and rebuild trust, Democrats must prioritize policies that address economic inequality while ensuring their advocacy for marginalized groups does not give the impression that broader economic struggles are secondary.

This does not mean abandoning the fight for racial, gender, or LGBTQ+ equality—these are fundamental issues of justice that must remain central to the party's platform. Instead, Democrats should present these struggles as part of a more extensive pursuit of fairness, opportunity, and dignity for everyone. They can build a coalition grounded in unity rather than division by highlighting the shared economic and social challenges that transcend identity lines.

The goal should be an inclusive vision—one that actively combats systemic discrimination while ensuring that working-class Americans of all backgrounds feel heard, valued, and represented.

A Vision for Economic Justice: Addressing Inequality and Creating Opportunity

MAGA's success in capturing the frustrations of working-class voters stems from its ability to frame economic hardship as the result of elite betrayal, globalization, and shifting cultural norms. By presenting Trump and his movement as champions of the "forgotten Americans," MAGA has cultivated a loyal base among those who feel alienated by economic changes and disillusioned with traditional political leadership. Meanwhile, Democrats have often struggled to offer a clear, emotionally resonant alternative that speaks directly to these voters. While Democratic policies frequently provide tangible economic benefits, such as support for unions, expanded healthcare access, and higher wages, the party's messaging has not always effectively connected these policies to the lived experiences of the working class. Instead, cultural issues have often overshadowed economic messaging, allowing MAGA to claim the mantle of economic populism despite advocating for policies that primarily benefit corporations and the wealthy.

To counter this narrative, Democrats must reframe the conversation around economic justice by emphasizing the material struggles facing all working Americans. This does not mean sidelining advocacy for marginalized communities, but rather integrating those concerns into a broader economic framework centered on fairness and opportunity for everyone. Too often, economic messaging has been drowned out by polarizing cultural debates that, while important, do not always resonate with voters whose primary concerns are financial stability, job security, and the rising cost of living. Democrats need to speak directly to these concerns by clearly showing how their policies will improve the everyday lives of all Americans.

A crucial component of this strategy is demonstrating that policies benefiting the middle and working class are not just aspirational ideals but necessary steps to reverse decades of economic inequality. The widening wealth gap, stagnant wages, and soaring costs of housing and healthcare have placed a growing burden on working-class Americans, especially in rural communities and former industrial hubs where jobs have vanished due to automation and globalization. Addressing these challenges requires more than technical policy tweaks; it demands a bold, populist economic vision matching MAGA's emotional appeal.

Policies such as raising the minimum wage, strengthening unions, and implementing universal healthcare are not only moral imperatives—they are political necessities if Democrats hope to reclaim their identity as the party of the working class.

Additionally, Democrats must directly challenge MAGA's narrative that economic decline stems primarily from immigration, diversity initiatives, or progressive social policies. This scapegoating deflects attention from the real drivers of inequality—corporate greed, tax policies that favor the wealthy, and deregulation that has weakened worker protections.

Democrats must emphasize that economic hardship is the result of deliberate policy decisions, such as tax cuts for billionaires, the outsourcing of jobs, and attacks on labor rights, not the presence of marginalized communities or government efforts to promote inclusion. By refocusing the debate on policies that materially improve people's lives, Democrats can undercut MAGA's misleading economic message and build a broader coalition of voters who understand that true economic justice uplifts everyone, not just the wealthy and well-connected.

At the same time, Democrats cannot overlook the role that social and identity-based issues play in shaping economic outcomes. Systemic barriers continue to disproportionately affect women, people of color, and LGBTQ+ individuals, making it essential to address these disparities within a broader economic justice framework. However, rather than presenting these concerns as separate from economic issues, Democrats should weave them into a unified message highlighting shared struggles and collective solutions. For instance, advocating for equal pay, expanding access to affordable childcare, and protecting worker rights across lines of race, gender, and immigration status should be positioned as part of a comprehensive economic agenda, not isolated social justice causes.

Ultimately, reclaiming the narrative on economic justice requires Democrats to be bold and unapologetic in their advocacy for working people. They must reject the false dichotomy that pits economic populism against social progressivism and show how both are essential to building a just and prosperous society. By making economic equity the foundation of their platform, while ensuring that social justice remains central to that vision, Democrats can begin to rebuild trust with working-class voters and offer a powerful alternative to MAGA's divisive and misleading brand of populism.

Rebuilding the Middle Class

For too long, the American middle class has faced stagnating wages, the disappearance of good-paying jobs, and the erosion of benefits that once defined economic stability. The political conversation has often been dominated by cultural and identity-based issues, leaving many working-class voters feeling as though their struggles have been sidelined. While MAGA has capitalized on this frustration—often through misleading narratives—Democrats must recognize that the most effective way to win back these voters is by focusing on policies that address their real economic concerns, including job creation, wage growth, and affordable healthcare. Economic security is the cornerstone of a thriving middle class. Without a compelling economic message, Democrats risk ceding ground to a movement that offers simplistic yet emotionally resonant explanations for economic hardship. To counter this, Democrats must strike a careful balance: advancing inclusive policies to uplift all Americans, primarily working-class communities.

1. Investing in Infrastructure

Democrats can build on the momentum of the Bipartisan Infrastructure Law by advocating for further investments in public infrastructure, renewable energy, and emerging technologies. These investments are more than just public works—they represent a transformative opportunity to create millions of good-paying jobs in communities nationwide. By focusing on green energy development, broadband expansion, and modernizing transportation systems, Democrats can ensure that the benefits of infrastructure investment reach both urban and rural areas. Too often, economic opportunities are concentrated in major metropolitan centers, leaving smaller towns and rural regions behind. Strategic investments in roads, bridges, public transit, water systems, and renewable energy projects can help reverse this trend and revitalize communities that have long suffered from deindustrialization and economic neglect.

These policies are not just about fixing roads or upgrading transit—they are about building pathways for workers to forge lasting careers in industries that will shape the future economy, from clean energy to digital infrastructure. When Democrats champion infrastructure investment, they help drive economic growth, reduce inequality, and create a more sustainable and inclusive economy. A well-planned infrastructure strategy also lowers business costs, boosts domestic production, and reduces reliance on fragile global supply chains. The long-term benefits of infrastructure spending extend well beyond job creation—they lay the foundation for an economy where workers and businesses can thrive.

2. Supporting Small Businesses and Local Economies

Unlike MAGA's corporate-friendly tax cuts, which overwhelmingly benefit large, multinational corporations, Democrats can focus on policies that empower small businesses and strengthen local economies. By expanding access to capital, providing incentives for community-based development, and supporting policies that promote local manufacturing and entrepreneurship, Democrats can help create jobs that stay within communities, boost regional stability, and provide hardworking families with the tools they need to succeed. Local businesses are more likely to reinvest in their neighborhoods, hire locally, and contribute to long-term economic resilience, whereas multinational corporations often prioritize profit margins over worker well-being.

A critical part of this strategy involves reforming predatory lending practices that disproportionately affect small businesses, particularly those owned by minorities, and expanding access to grants and low-interest loans to support new business creation. Additionally, promoting "Buy American" initiatives and offering targeted incentives to companies that manufacture domestically can help revive industries hollowed out by decades of outsourcing. Economic nationalism does not have to be a MAGA talking point—Democrats can reclaim it by demonstrating that smart, targeted investments in American workers and small businesses create a fairer, stronger economy.

3. Raising the Minimum Wage and Strengthening Labor Unions

A more equitable economy demands a fairer distribution of wealth. Raising the federal minimum wage to at least $15 per hour and supporting unionization efforts are essential steps toward achieving that goal. A living wage is not a luxury—it is a necessity that allows workers to support their families, invest in their communities, and live with dignity. As inflation rises and the cost of living increases across cities and rural areas, stagnant wages have left millions of Americans struggling to make ends meet.

Strengthening labor unions is equally important, as unions have long been vital in improving working conditions and securing fair pay. Decades of corporate-backed efforts to weaken unions have eroded workers' bargaining power, leading to lower wages, fewer benefits, and reduced job security. By supporting legislation like the PRO Act, Democrats can help restore workers' rights to organize and negotiate for better wages, benefits, and protections. States with stronger unions tend to have higher wages, safer working conditions, and lower economic inequality, making labor reform a cornerstone of rebuilding the middle class.

These policies are about building an economy prioritizing people over profits and delivering greater financial security and opportunity for all Americans. The labor movement has always been a driving force behind progress. Democrats must continue to fight for policies that protect workers from corporate exploitation while ensuring that every job offers fair pay and dignified conditions.

4. Fair Taxation and Closing Loopholes

The U.S. tax system is intended to be progressive, requiring higher-income individuals and corporations to pay higher rates. However, various loopholes, deductions, and tax avoidance strategies have allowed the wealthiest Americans and large corporations to significantly reduce their tax obligations, shifting a disproportionate financial burden onto middle- and working-class Americans. While MAGA Republicans often claim to champion the working class, their tax policies have overwhelmingly favored the ultra-wealthy. The 2017 Tax Cuts and Jobs Act (TCJA), championed by President Donald Trump, reduced the corporate tax rate from 35% to 21%, delivering the most significant benefits to large corporations and the top 1%, while offering only temporary and modest relief to middle- and lower-income earners. The law has been widely criticized for deepening income inequality and causing substantial losses in federal revenue that could have otherwise supported public services and infrastructure.

Instead of overhauling the entire tax system, Democrats should pursue targeted reforms that strengthen their progressive structure and ensure billionaires and multinational corporations pay their fair share. One essential step is implementing a corporate minimum tax. The Inflation Reduction Act introduced a 15% corporate alternative minimum tax (CAMT) on the adjusted financial statement income of large corporations earning over $1 billion annually. This policy is expected to raise substantial revenue over the next decade (Internal Revenue Service, n.d.; National Law Review, 2022; CRS Products, 2022).

Another key reform involves addressing how wealth is taxed. In the U.S., wealth is increasingly accumulated through investments rather than wages, enabling the wealthiest Americans to benefit from lower capital gains tax rates. Raising capital gains taxes on high earners and imposing a tax on stock buybacks would help ensure that investment income is taxed more equitably and could yield significant revenue (Inequality.org, 2025).

Cracking down on offshore tax havens is equally critical. Multinational corporations often shift profits overseas to avoid paying U.S. taxes, costing the federal government billions. Stronger regulations on international corporate earnings could recapture lost revenue and ensure that corporations contribute more to the domestic economy from which they profit.

Balancing the need for increased revenue with maintaining a competitive business environment is essential. A modest increase in corporate tax rates could raise funds without incentivizing companies to relocate abroad. At the same time, offering tax incentives for domestic manufacturing, research and development, and job creation would encourage companies to invest at home.

Strengthening IRS enforcement is another necessary step. Tax evasion by the wealthiest individuals and corporations costs the U.S. hundreds of billions annually. Increasing funding for IRS audits and investigations could recover substantial revenue without burdening middle-income taxpayers.

Closing loopholes and ensuring fair taxation could generate significant new revenue for reinvestment in healthcare, education, infrastructure, and housing. Unlike MAGA tax cuts, which increased the deficit without meaningfully benefiting working Americans, targeted tax reforms would support long-term economic growth by investing in people and communities. Rather than pushing broad, across-the-board tax increases, Democrats should frame these reforms as economic fairness and accountability, ensuring the wealthiest individuals and corporations pay their fair share. Hence, the economy works for everyone, not just the privileged few.

5. Affordable Housing and Education

Affordable housing and access to quality education are two of the most urgent challenges facing the American middle class. Soaring rents and home prices have made homeownership increasingly out of reach, while mounting student loan debt has hindered financial stability for millions. Addressing these issues is not just about helping low-income families but preventing middle-class households from slipping into economic insecurity.

To ensure long-term stability, Democrats must prioritize expanding affordable housing initiatives, increasing investment in public education, and addressing the student debt crisis. Strengthening federal housing programs, enforcing tenant protections, and incentivizing local governments to build more affordable units can help keep housing accessible for working families. Likewise, reducing college costs and expanding access to trade and vocational schools can offer more affordable and practical pathways to economic mobility, ensuring higher education is not an insurmountable financial burden.

By tackling these issues, Democrats can help ensure that all Americans, regardless of race, class, or background, have access to safe, affordable housing and the educational opportunities necessary for advancement. These policies do not just benefit individuals; they strengthen the broader economy by boosting homeownership, reducing financial stress, and equipping more people to contribute meaningfully to society.

Addressing the economic challenges MAGA rhetoric often exploits gives Democrats a powerful opportunity to offer a forward-looking vision of shared prosperity and real economic justice. By focusing on infrastructure, small businesses, fair wages, equitable taxation, and long-term stability, Democrats can present a compelling alternative to MAGA's false promises and divisive culture war distractions. To reclaim the narrative, they must reassert themselves as the party of economic progress, committed to protecting and expanding the middle class through bold, inclusive, and equitable policies.

A Vision for Social Justice: Fighting for Racial, Gender, and LGBTQ+ Equality

Democrats must continue championing racial, gender, and LGBTQ+ justice. However, they must also ensure these issues are woven into a broader conversation about all working-class Americans' economic challenges. Many voters, particularly in economically distressed areas, feel alienated when identity-based issues dominate the political discourse while their financial struggles, such as low wages, job insecurity, unaffordable healthcare, and rising living costs, go unaddressed. When economic concerns are sidelined in favor of policies focused primarily on identity categories, working-class voters of all backgrounds may feel overlooked, fueling resentment that MAGA Republicans have successfully exploited.

Rather than dismissing this frustration as reactionary, Democrats must acknowledge that economic stress is a key driver of the discontent that draws many voters toward MAGA populism.

To bridge this divide, Democrats must embrace a more inclusive vision of social justice that upholds marginalized communities' rights while framing economic justice as a shared struggle. The fight for racial, gender, and LGBTQ+ equality should not be treated as separate from economic reform but as integral to ensuring fairness and opportunity for all. Stagnant wages, limited job opportunities, and skyrocketing living costs affect people across racial, gender, and geographic lines. By linking social justice with broad economic reform, Democrats can strengthen their connection with voters who might otherwise feel disconnected from the party's priorities. This approach does not weaken the commitment to marginalized communities—it strengthens it by showing that social and economic justice are inseparable.

For too long, Republicans have successfully portrayed Democrats as a party consumed by identity politics while casting themselves as defenders of the "forgotten" working class. This narrative is misleading—MAGA policies overwhelmingly benefit the wealthy and corporate elite—but it resonates because Democrats have not always countered it effectively. Rather than letting Republicans frame the debate, Democrats must reassert social justice as part of a broader fight for economic fairness. Policies like expanding labor rights, ensuring equal pay, and strengthening the social safety net should not be presented as niche initiatives for select groups—they should be framed as central to improving life for all working-class Americans.

Integrating economic policy into the social justice conversation also creates opportunities to build coalitions across communities. Black, Latino, white, LGBTQ+, and rural voters all experience financial hardship, even if the nature of that hardship varies. A platform centered on job creation, universal healthcare, and affordable housing sends a unifying message: the root causes of inequality must be addressed systemically, not through narrowly targeted cultural policies, but through comprehensive reform that lifts everyone. By shifting the focus from divisive culture wars to tangible economic solutions, Democrats can present a compelling vision of shared prosperity that is both inclusive and electorally powerful.

There is no question that racial, gender, and LGBTQ+ discrimination remain urgent problems demanding action. However, to build broad support, Democrats must show how addressing these issues benefits all Americans. For example, raising the minimum wage and strengthening labor protections disproportionately help women and communities of color, who are overrepresented in low-wage jobs. Expanding healthcare access aids LGBTQ+ individuals, who often face discrimination in medical settings, while also serving rural Americans struggling with hospital closures. When Democrats present these policies as universally beneficial rather than identity-specific, they make the case that social justice is not about elevating one group over another but securing dignity, equity, and opportunity for everyone.

At the same time, Democrats must be cautious of performative activism that fails to address structural inequalities. Symbolic gestures—such as corporate diversity statements or changes to brand logos—do not create meaningful progress. In many cases, they provoke backlash by reinforcing the perception that Democrats are more concerned with political correctness than substantive economic policy. Instead, the party should prioritize policies that tangibly improve people's lives. This means advocating for strong labor protections, expanding access to public education, investing in historically marginalized communities, and ensuring that all Americans, regardless of race, gender, or sexual orientation, have a fair shot at economic stability.

Democrats have a unique opportunity to unite Americans across racial and cultural divides by focusing on policies that enhance everyone's economic well-being. Raising the minimum wage, expanding healthcare access, investing in education, and strengthening worker protections are widely supported measures that resonate across demographics. By emphasizing these priorities, Democrats can show that their fight for justice is about improving the lives of all Americans, not just specific groups. Economic justice is social justice, and framing it this way allows Democrats to push back against the notion that identity politics eclipses the everyday struggles of working families.

By reclaiming the economic narrative and making working-class concerns central to social justice discussions, Democrats can build a more unifying and hopeful political platform rooted in fairness, opportunity, and prosperity for all. Rather than letting MAGA forces divide voters along cultural lines, Democrats must offer a bold, forward-looking agenda that links social progress to economic advancement. If they succeed, they can reshape the political landscape, win back disillusioned voters, and help fulfill the promise of America for everyone, not just the privileged few.

Fighting for Racial Justice

Racial inequality remains a critical issue in America, but Democrats must ensure their approach to addressing it does not unintentionally alienate working-class voters who also face significant economic hardship. While systemic racism must be acknowledged and confronted, the way these discussions are framed can sometimes make struggling white, working-class Americans feel as though their challenges are being overlooked. This has given MAGA Republicans an opening to exploit economic anxieties and racial resentment for political gain. Democrats must push back by making it clear that racial justice is not about prioritizing one group over another—it is about guaranteeing fairness, opportunity, and dignity for everyone.

By emphasizing policies that uplift all workers, such as raising the minimum wage, expanding access to affordable healthcare, and investing in public education, Democrats can simultaneously address racial and economic inequality. Framing racial justice efforts as part of a broader movement for shared prosperity strengthens multiracial solidarity and makes it harder for conservatives to weaponize racial divisions to derail progressive goals.

1. Criminal Justice Reform

Policing in America remains a deeply contentious issue, as systemic racism and police brutality continue to fuel national protests and political debate. The killing of unarmed Black Americans, the over-policing of marginalized communities, and the use of excessive force underscore the urgent need for comprehensive criminal justice reform. While Republicans often lean on public safety fears to justify over-policing, Democrats must advocate for policies that promote safety and justice.

Reforms like banning chokeholds, ending racial profiling, and implementing stronger accountability measures for law enforcement are essential to restoring trust between communities and the police. Democrats should also champion alternative public safety models, including community-based policing and expanded mental health crisis response teams, which can reduce the likelihood of violent encounters. The emphasis should be on reallocating resources to evidence-based strategies that enhance public safety for all, not on the politically fraught phrase "defund the police," which has often overshadowed the substance of reform efforts.

Mass incarceration is another urgent issue, mainly because it disproportionately impacts Black and Latino Americans. The United States incarcerates more people than any other country, often for nonviolent offenses that could be better addressed through rehabilitation rather than imprisonment. Democrats should prioritize sentencing reform, ending the use of private prisons, and expanding opportunities for record expungement. These changes would address racial disparities within the justice system and support the successful reintegration of formerly incarcerated individuals, empowering them to rebuild their lives and contribute meaningfully to their communities.

2. Addressing Systemic Inequality

Rather than ignoring America's long history of racial injustice or downplaying its ongoing impact on communities of color, Democrats must lead with both honesty and concrete solutions. Addressing systemic inequality should not be framed around guilt or division, but around enacting practical policies that rectify long-standing disparities. Targeted investments in historically Black and Latino communities, expanded homeownership programs, and equitable funding for public schools serving minority populations are necessary steps toward closing the racial wealth gap. These initiatives should be framed as economic investments that strengthen all communities, not as zero-sum redistribution.

While politically controversial, reparations deserve serious discussion, not as a radical demand, but as a pragmatic solution to address the long-term economic effects of racial discrimination. Though direct cash payments face considerable opposition, particularly from white middle-class voters whose support is crucial for Democrats, a more politically viable strategy would focus on grant-based programs that build sustainable wealth. Expanding access to homeownership through down payment assistance and low-interest loans could help close the racial housing gap while minimizing political backlash. Similarly, increasing federal funding for HBCUs, broadening Pell Grant eligibility, and implementing targeted student debt relief for marginalized communities would provide long-term pathways to economic mobility. Business development grants and expanded access to capital for minority entrepreneurs would further support wealth creation and job growth.

Closing the racial wealth gap must be a national priority. Today, the median white household holds roughly eight times the wealth of the median Black household, and five times that of the median Latino household—a disparity rooted in historical policies such as redlining, wage discrimination, and exclusion from federal benefits. Addressing this requires a multi-pronged approach: strengthening legal protections against housing discrimination, boosting funding for fair housing enforcement, and holding financial institutions accountable for discriminatory lending practices. Supporting community development financial institutions (CDFIs) and creating a national investment fund for minority-owned businesses would provide the resources to break systemic financial barriers.

To successfully pass these policies, Democrats must frame them as investments in shared prosperity rather than race-exclusive benefits. Republicans have long weaponized racial resentment to convince white working-class voters that racial justice policies come at their expense. To counter this narrative, programs like homeownership and business grants should also be designed to assist low-income white families, while still prioritizing the needs of communities of color who have faced generations of exclusion.

Reparations should not be viewed as financial handouts but as strategic investments in economic empowerment. By focusing on grants for homeownership, education, and business development, alongside broader economic policies that uplift all working-class families, Democrats can work toward racial equity without alienating key voter blocs. The objective is to acknowledge past injustices and create meaningful, lasting pathways to generational wealth that benefit entire communities. Investing in historically marginalized groups strengthens the economy and reinforces the truth that racial and economic justice are deeply interconnected.

Championing Gender Equality and LGBTQ+ Rights

The fight for gender equality and LGBTQ+ rights remains critical, but how these issues are framed often determines their political effectiveness. MAGA Republicans have successfully portrayed progress in these areas as an attack on traditional values, stoking fears that social change is being forced upon unwilling Americans. Democrats must counter this narrative by making clear that gender and LGBTQ+ equality are not isolated cultural battles, but are deeply connected to economic opportunity, personal freedom, and workplace protections—issues that affect all Americans. Rather than allowing these rights to be dismissed as "woke" distractions, Democrats should frame them as essential to a fair and functioning democracy. A country where everyone can work without discrimination, access healthcare without political interference, and make decisions about their bodies without government intrusion upholds true freedom and stability for all.

At the same time, it is important to recognize that overemphasizing these issues in ways that feel disconnected from broader concerns, such as job security, inflation, and healthcare, can alienate voters who feel their struggles are overlooked. This does not mean stepping back from the fight for equality, but embedding gender and LGBTQ+ rights within a larger vision of shared prosperity. By showing how these policies contribute to economic stability, enhance personal freedoms, and support middle-class families, Democrats can neutralize right-wing fearmongering while expanding their coalition.

1. Protecting Reproductive Rights

The Supreme Court's decision to overturn Roe v. Wade was not just a rollback of women's rights—it was an economic catastrophe for millions of women and families. Restricting access to abortion disproportionately affects low-income women, rural communities, and young people who lack the financial means to travel to states where reproductive care remains legal. These bans worsen cycles of poverty, forcing individuals to carry pregnancies they may not be financially or emotionally prepared for, increasing the likelihood of job loss, economic instability, and reliance on public assistance. Additionally, maternal mortality rates—already disproportionately high for Black and Indigenous women—are expected to rise as abortion access declines, further straining public health systems.

Democrats must emphasize that reproductive freedom is not only a moral issue—it is also a matter of economic justice and personal liberty. Without the ability to make decisions about their bodies, women face more significant financial hardship, increased workplace discrimination, and limited career advancement. In states with strict abortion bans, employers may hesitate to hire women of childbearing age due to concerns about healthcare costs and potential workforce disruptions. This dynamic reinforces the fact that reproductive rights are inseparable from economic opportunity, and Democrats should make that connection clear.

To regain lost ground, Democrats should advocate for federal protections of reproductive rights while also promoting access to contraception, paid parental leave, and stronger maternal healthcare policies. Framing the issue in this broader context ensures that reproductive rights are seen not just as a cultural or moral concern, but as central to the economic security of working families. Moreover, by highlighting how abortion restrictions harm economic growth—by pushing women out of the workforce, increasing dependence on social programs, and overburdening healthcare systems—Democrats can counter conservative narratives that dismiss reproductive rights as fringe issues.

Beyond legal protections, Democrats should also invest in reproductive health education and services. Comprehensive sex education and affordable contraception are proven tools for reducing unintended pregnancies, making them practical, widely beneficial policy solutions. By positioning reproductive rights as part of a broader commitment to healthcare access and economic well-being, Democrats can shift the conversation away from partisan division and toward common-sense solutions that resonate with a broad range of voters.

2. Strengthening Workplace Protections and Economic Security

MAGA Republicans claim to be pro-worker, yet they consistently oppose policies that ensure fair treatment in the workplace. While culture war rhetoric dominates right-wing media, many Americans, regardless of their personal views on gender and LGBTQ+ issues, support policies that protect against workplace discrimination, ensure equal pay, and expand family leave. Democrats must seize this opportunity by making workplace protections a central pillar of their economic agenda.

More vigorous enforcement against sexual harassment, pay disparities, and wrongful termination must be a priority. Women and LGBTQ+ workers continue to face disproportionate levels of workplace discrimination, yet current federal protections contain significant loopholes. The wage gap remains a persistent issue, especially for women of color and transgender individuals, who often earn significantly less than white, cisgender men. Strengthening equal pay laws, increasing penalties for workplace discrimination, and requiring greater transparency in corporate pay structures are essential steps toward achieving economic justice.

Additionally, expanding paid family leave, raising the minimum wage, and ensuring access to affordable childcare benefits not just women and LGBTQ+ workers, but all working Americans. The United States remains one of the few developed nations without guaranteed paid family leave, forcing many parents, particularly mothers, to choose between their jobs and caregiving responsibilities. Meanwhile, affordable childcare remains out of reach for many families, making it harder for parents to maintain steady employment. Democrats should emphasize how these policies boost workforce participation, increase productivity, and help businesses attract and retain talent. Framing these initiatives as economic imperatives—not just social justice goals—can help win over voters who might otherwise be skeptical.

LGBTQ+ workers, in particular, face unique economic challenges, including higher rates of job discrimination and limited access to employer-provided benefits. In many states without explicit workplace protections, LGBTQ+ employees still fear being fired for their identity. Moreover, many employer-based health plans fail to cover essential transgender healthcare services, leaving trans workers without access to necessary medical care. While Republicans often dismiss LGBTQ+ rights as matters of personal belief, Democrats must make clear that workplace discrimination carries actual economic costs. Ensuring federal protections for LGBTQ+ workers strengthens the economy by ensuring talent is not wasted due to prejudice or exclusion.

3. Expanding LGBTQ+ Rights Through Legal and Economic Protections

The rapid spread of anti-LGBTQ+ legislation—from "Don't Say Gay" laws to bans on gender-affirming care—reflects a coordinated effort by the right to roll back personal freedoms under the guise of protecting children and "traditional values." These policies are not only harmful to LGBTQ+ individuals but also set a dangerous precedent of government overreach. While Republicans often claim to defend personal liberty, they have weaponized government power to restrict speech, control medical decisions, and dictate how individuals live their lives. Democrats must challenge these laws not only as civil rights violations but also as fundamental threats to individual freedom and economic stability.

Rather than allowing LGBTQ+ rights to be portrayed as fringe concerns, Democrats should demonstrate how attacks on these freedoms ultimately harm society as a whole. When transgender individuals are denied access to healthcare, the burden shifts to emergency rooms and social services. Studies show that states enacting anti-LGBTQ+ laws often face economic backlash, as businesses and significant events relocate to more inclusive environments. Corporations increasingly oppose discriminatory policies, recognizing that an inclusive workforce is vital for innovation and long-term growth. When LGBTQ+ youth face discrimination in schools, their educational and economic prospects decline, reducing both workforce participation and potential. Moreover, local economies suffer when companies operating in conservative states experience pushback over restrictive laws. By highlighting these impacts, Democrats can appeal to a broader audience beyond those directly affected.

Democrats should also take a proactive approach to protecting LGBTQ+ rights at the federal level, advocating for comprehensive anti-discrimination legislation across employment, housing, healthcare, and education. However, this must be done to prevent Republicans from framing these protections as special privileges. The message should be clear: no American should be denied opportunity or dignity because of who they are. LGBTQ+ rights are not about forcing social change—they are about ensuring everyone can live without fear of being denied a job, a home, or medical care due to their identity.

Additionally, Democrats must confront the growing violence and harassment targeting LGBTQ+ individuals, particularly transgender Americans. The rise in hate crimes and coordinated attacks on LGBTQ+ spaces is no coincidence—it stems from dehumanizing, inflammatory right-wing rhetoric. Stronger legal protections against hate crimes, improved law enforcement training to address bias-motivated violence, and increased funding for LGBTQ+ community centers must all be part of a comprehensive push for equality and safety.

Ultimately, Democrats must not allow Republicans to dictate the terms of this debate. LGBTQ+ rights are not a niche concern—they are about whether all Americans can live free from government interference, workplace discrimination, and violence. By framing the fight for equality as a fight for personal liberty, economic opportunity, and societal stability, Democrats can reclaim the narrative and offer a compelling vision of an America that is genuinely free and inclusive for all.

A Vision for Responsible Immigration: Lawful Pathways and Fair Enforcement

Immigration has long been a cornerstone of the American story. Generations of newcomers have arrived in the United States seeking freedom, opportunity, and stability—values that remain central to the nation's identity. From building railroads and revitalizing communities to driving innovation and entrepreneurship, immigrants have played a vital role in shaping the American economy and culture. At the same time, any country that aims to manage immigration effectively must strike a careful balance between welcoming newcomers and upholding the rule of law.

Today's immigration debate too often falls into extremes. On one side, immigration is reduced to a national security issue, as though the millions of undocumented individuals contributing to society pose a threat to the nation's core. On the other hand, calls for reform are sometimes mischaracterized as disregarding border control. This binary framing is unproductive. It overlooks the complexity of immigration policy and fails to reflect what most Americans want: a secure, orderly, and fair system.

Democrats can present a vision that rises above the political noise, rooted in responsibility, humanity, and respect for the law. That means acknowledging the real challenges posed by illegal immigration while resisting the impulse to rely on rhetoric or reactionary policies. A secure border and a compassionate approach are not opposing goals but complementary parts of a functional immigration system.

Illegal immigration should not be ignored or excused. Clear and enforceable laws are necessary to protect the integrity of the immigration system and maintain public trust. However, enforcement should focus on addressing genuine threats and upholding legal processes, not on implementing broad, punitive measures that treat all undocumented individuals as criminals. Most undocumented immigrants are not malicious actors; many are workers, parents, and neighbors who contribute to their communities but lack a path to legal status due to an outdated and overwhelmed system.

Improving legal immigration channels is a critical component of meaningful reform. Many individuals and families attempting to immigrate legally face arbitrary quotas, decades-long wait times, and a maze of bureaucracy. When legal pathways are blocked or inaccessible, people are more likely to pursue unauthorized routes, mainly when fleeing violence, corruption, or extreme poverty. A fair and modernized immigration system would help reduce illegal crossings by providing viable legal alternatives.

In addition to improving the legal process, enforcement must be strategic and focused. Immigration policy should prioritize identifying and removing individuals who pose legitimate security risks, not tearing apart families or destabilizing industries that depend on immigrant labor. A more innovative approach, grounded in modern technology and interagency coordination, can secure the border without resorting to overly punitive policies that instill fear and uncertainty.

This is not about ignoring the law or abandoning enforcement. It is about building a system that works—one that secures the border, upholds the rule of law, and reflects America's values of fairness and opportunity. A responsible immigration agenda must also look beyond the border. Addressing the root causes of migration, such as poverty, violence, and political instability in countries of origin, can ease pressure at the border and show that the United States is committed to long-term solutions, not just short-term fixes.

A nation built by immigrants should not treat immigration as a threat, but as a challenge to be managed wisely and fairly. This vision does not call for open borders or endorse the status quo. It recognizes that real reform requires seriousness, discipline, and empathy, essential to restoring credibility to the immigration system. Democrats should lead with a message that rejects false choices. The United States can protect its borders while remaining true to its legacy as a land of opportunity. Responsible immigration policy is more than a political stance—it reflects national values and a belief that security and compassion can, and must, coexist.

1. Security and Compassion Can Coexist

In today's political climate, immigration debates are too often reduced to false choices—security versus compassion, enforcement versus openness. This framing benefits those who aim to shut down reform efforts entirely. The claim that Democrats support "open borders" is not based in reality, yet it is frequently repeated to portray any attempt to modernize the immigration system as radical or dangerous. In truth, Democrats can—and should—clarify that upholding the rule of law is essential. Illegal immigration presents real logistical, legal, and economic challenges. However, securing the border does not require abandoning America's commitment to fairness and human dignity.

Much of the current enforcement debate has centered on past policies that led to family separations and prolonged detentions in substandard conditions. Regardless of intention, the outcomes of these policies have raised serious concerns about the moral cost of specific enforcement strategies. Often justified as deterrence, these approaches have proven ineffective in addressing long-term migration trends and have damaged America's global reputation. Enforcement driven by punishment rather than precision ignores the root causes of illegal immigration—causes that cannot be resolved through fear-based policies alone.

Democrats can shift this conversation toward a more innovative, more targeted approach. Immigration enforcement should prioritize individuals who pose legitimate security risks, such as those involved in criminal activity or trafficking, rather than casting broad nets that ensnare workers, families, and asylum seekers. Many who cross the border without authorization are fleeing life-threatening conditions, not seeking to exploit the system. While the law must be upheld, it should be enforced in ways that reflect American values and differentiate between dangerous actors and those seeking survival or opportunity.

Rejecting the false choice between compassion and enforcement is essential. A functional system must do both. By advocating for clear rules that are pretty and humanely enforced, Democrats can demonstrate that border security and human dignity are not opposing goals. Each is incomplete without the other.

2. Fixing the Legal Immigration System

Any honest discussion about unauthorized immigration must begin with the acknowledgment that the legal immigration system is outdated and often unworkable. Many who come to the United States illegally do so not out of disregard for the law, but because current pathways to lawful entry are riddled with obstacles. Arbitrary quotas, years-long wait times, and bureaucratic inefficiencies make it extremely difficult for many to pursue legal immigration, even when they have compelling economic or humanitarian reasons.

This dysfunction affects more than would-be immigrants. It strains border resources, incentivizes unauthorized entry, and harms American industries that rely on immigrant labor. When people lack legal avenues to fill labor shortages or seek asylum through a timely and fair process, illegal crossings become a last resort. Improving legal pathways would relieve pressure at the border and allow immigration enforcement to focus more effectively on genuine security threats.

Reform should include expanding employment-based visa programs in high-demand agriculture, healthcare, and technology sectors. These changes would support economic growth while reducing the incentive for unauthorized immigration. The asylum system also requires urgent attention. A massive backlog of cases has left countless people in limbo, undermining the system's credibility and creating conditions ripe for abuse. A functional asylum process must be timely, thorough, and just, ensuring that those with valid claims receive protection while preventing the system from being overwhelmed.

The broader immigration system must also be modernized to reflect current labor market demands and demographic realities. Many immigrants wait decades to reunite with family or secure employment-based visas. These delays are not only inefficient but also inhumane. The United States can maintain control over its borders by streamlining bureaucratic processes and updating outdated laws while benefiting from new arrivals' economic and cultural contributions.

By taking the lead on legal immigration reform, Democrats can also neutralize one of the right wing's most persistent talking points: that the system is chaotic and unmanageable. A fairer, more efficient, and accessible legal immigration system would reduce unauthorized crossings, enhance labor market stability, and reassure voters that America still values immigration, but is committed to doing it correctly.

3. Improving Immigration Enforcement Without Fearmongering

Immigration enforcement is a necessary component of any functioning system, but how it is carried out matters deeply. Calls for mass deportations or broad, sweeping enforcement measures may appeal to a desire for order, but in practice, these approaches often backfire—both morally and practically. The vast majority of undocumented immigrants are not violent criminals. Many have lived in the U.S. for years, paid taxes, raised families, and contributed meaningfully to their communities. Treating them as threats to national security undermines the credibility of enforcement policies and alienates key segments of the public.

Enforcement strategies should reflect the complexity of the issue. Prioritizing the deportation of individuals who pose legitimate security threats, rather than engaging in indiscriminate removals, allows immigration authorities to focus their resources more effectively. Likewise, investing in modern border technology, improving screening at legal ports of entry, and enhancing data-sharing across agencies will do more to strengthen national security than symbolic or punitive measures like constructing a border wall.

Democrats should also emphasize long-term strategies that address the root causes of migration. Many individuals come to the United States fleeing political instability, economic collapse, or violence in their home countries. Increased investment in foreign aid and development programs—particularly in Central America—can help build safer, more prosperous societies, reducing the pressure to migrate. This approach is not about opening borders but about giving people a reason to stay in their home countries. It is a humane and cost-effective way to manage migration flows over the long term.

Finally, Democrats must actively push back against fear-based narratives that dominate the immigration debate. Claims that immigrants are responsible for increased crime, economic decline, or cultural erosion are not supported by evidence. In reality, immigrant communities contribute significantly to the U.S. economy, pay billions in taxes, and commit crimes at lower rates than native-born citizens. However, misinformation will continue to fill the void if these facts are not communicated clearly and consistently.

By advocating for firm, focused, and fair enforcement policies and rejecting fearmongering, Democrats can reframe the immigration conversation. A secure and humane immigration system is not a contradiction but the foundation of responsible reform. The path forward does not lie in extremes but in recognizing that lawful enforcement and national compassion must go hand in hand.

A Vision for National Unity: Building a Politics of Hope, Not Fear

A thriving democracy depends on a shared sense of purpose—the belief that, despite our differences, Americans are united by shared values and aspirations. Throughout history, the nation's most outstanding achievements have come through collective action, not division. The civil rights movement, the expansion of public education, the New Deal, and even the space race all testify to a country that embraced unity in pursuit of progress. However, the MAGA political strategy thrives on fear, resentment, and a manufactured sense of national decline, pitting communities against one another to maintain power. Rather than allowing this divisive rhetoric to dominate the national conversation, Democrats must present a compelling alternative that champions unity, resilience, and progress.

MAGA leaders exploit real economic and social frustrations, using them to scapegoat rather than solve. Instead of addressing the root causes of wage stagnation, declining rural economies, and the rising cost of living, they deflect blame onto immigrants, diversity initiatives, and evolving social norms. This deliberate misdirection distracts from policies that overwhelmingly benefit the wealthiest elites while leaving working-class Americans behind. Democrats must expose this deception and offer substantive solutions that tackle the authentic sources of economic hardship.

However, unity does not mean uniformity. Rather than viewing demographic and cultural change as a threat, Democrats must emphasize that diversity strengthens the nation. A society that welcomes people from varied backgrounds fosters innovation, adaptability, and economic vitality. From immigrants who built industries to activists who expanded civil rights to workers who powered economic growth, America's success has always relied on contributions from every walk of life. Elevating this narrative is essential to countering MAGA's attempts to portray diversity as a liability rather than an asset.

MAGA rhetoric often portrays progress toward inclusion as a loss for "traditional" Americans, promoting a false, zero-sum mentality. Democrats must reject this framing by showing how policies that uplift marginalized communities benefit everyone, such as fair wages, expanded healthcare, and stronger worker protections. A more inclusive economy creates broader opportunities and greater prosperity. History demonstrates that when barriers to participation are removed, economic mobility increases. Whether through the inclusion of women in the workforce, the desegregation of schools, or the expansion of civil rights, America has always thrived when it embraced progress rather than resisted it.

Still, words alone will not persuade voters who feel left behind by economic change and political dysfunction. Unity must be demonstrated through policies that deliver accurate results. Too often, MAGA politicians claim to represent the working class while advancing agendas that primarily serve the wealthy. Democrats must expose this contradiction and champion policies that materially improve the lives of all Americans, regardless of geography, race, or political affiliation.

At the core of this agenda must be a commitment to reducing economic inequality. Raising the minimum wage, expanding affordable healthcare, strengthening labor unions, and investing in public education all directly benefit working-class Americans from every background. Likewise, prioritizing initiatives such as universal broadband, infrastructure development, and rural revitalization will ensure economic opportunity reaches every corner of the country, not just urban centers.

Equally crucial to economic justice is the health of democracy itself. When people believe the political system is rigged against them, they become more susceptible to the resentment-driven politics on which MAGA depends. Democrats must push back against voter suppression, extreme gerrymandering, and the corrupting influence of dark money in politics. Restoring trust in democracy requires ensuring every American has a meaningful voice in shaping the nation's future. Only then can unity become more than a slogan—it can be a shared reality.

Strengthening Democracy and Electoral Integrity

A government that genuinely represents the people requires an electoral system that is fair, transparent, and accessible to all. However, structural barriers—from voter suppression tactics to the influence of big money in politics—have eroded public trust in democracy, disproportionately silencing marginalized communities. MAGA Republicans have not merely tolerated these inequities; they have actively worked to deepen them. Their goal is to entrench power in the hands of a select few while discouraging millions from participating. Democrats must make strengthening democracy a central pillar of their agenda, not simply in response to Republican efforts to undermine voting rights, but as a fundamental commitment to ensuring that every American has a voice in shaping the nation's future.

1. Protecting Voting Rights

Voting is not a privilege; it is a fundamental right that underpins democracy itself. However, this right is under constant attack from Republican-led efforts to restrict access to the ballot. Voter ID laws, aggressive purges of voter rolls, and limitations on early and mail-in voting disproportionately impact communities of color, low-income voters, and young people. These measures are not designed to protect election integrity but to determine who gets to participate in the democratic process selectively. The objective is clear: limit the electorate in ways that favor Republican candidates while suppressing voices that challenge their agenda.

The fight against voter suppression is not only about ensuring fair elections—it is about defending the very legitimacy of democracy. A government that does not reflect the people's will cannot function effectively or maintain public trust. That is why Democrats must oppose restrictive voting laws and actively champion policies that expand access to the ballot. Automatic voter registration, nationwide early voting, and same-day registration should be standard practices in all states. Restoring voting rights to formerly incarcerated individuals is also critical to addressing the long history of disenfranchisement that disproportionately affects Black and brown communities.

Gerrymandering remains one of the most insidious tools for manipulating electoral outcomes. By drawing districts that all but guarantee partisan victories, politicians effectively choose their voters instead of allowing voters to choose their representatives. This practice dilutes the power of individual votes and leaves many communities, especially communities of color, with little influence over policy decisions that directly affect their lives. Democrats must advocate for independent redistricting commissions and fair districting laws to ensure election outcomes genuinely reflect the electorate's will.

Beyond legislation, Democrats must frame voting rights as a matter of fundamental fairness and democratic integrity, not merely a partisan issue. By emphasizing that a more vigorous democracy benefits everyone, regardless of political affiliation, they can appeal to a broad coalition of voters, including independents and moderate conservatives who value free and fair elections. Ensuring that every voice is heard is not just a Democratic priority but an American imperative.

2. Reforming Campaign Finance

A democracy where political influence can be bought and sold is no democracy at all. The influx of corporate money into politics has deepened public cynicism and reinforced the perception that politicians serve their donors rather than the people. The Citizens United ruling opened the floodgates for unlimited campaign spending by corporations and special interest groups, drowning out the voices of everyday Americans and shifting power away from voters and toward the wealthiest elites.

This system does not just skew election outcomes—it distorts policymaking. When corporate lobbyists hold more sway than constituents, legislation reflects the interests of billionaires and multinational corporations rather than those of working families. This dynamic fuels economic inequality, weakens labor protections, and undermines environmental regulations—all because those with money can buy political outcomes that serve their financial interests.

Democrats must prioritize campaign finance reform as a foundational step toward restoring democracy. Overturning Citizens United should be a central objective, but reform efforts must go further. Implementing stricter disclosure requirements for political spending would ensure that dark money groups cannot flood elections with anonymous, corporate-backed advertisements. Expanding public financing of campaigns would give grassroots candidates a fair shot against well-funded opponents, leveling the playing field and enabling more diverse voices to enter politics.

Transparency is key. Voters deserve to know who is funding the candidates they are being asked to support. A system that favors billionaires and corporate PACs over working-class Americans is not sustainable. Democrats must make the case that real political power belongs in the hands of the people, not in the wallets of a wealthy few.

A National Narrative of Shared Purpose

Rather than falling into the trap of divisive identity politics, Democrats have the opportunity to build a narrative of shared purpose—one that unites all Americans around common goals and collective progress. The country stands at a crossroads, where the politics of division and fear, championed by the MAGA movement, threaten to tear apart the fabric of American democracy. Democrats can counter this by emphasizing the values and aspirations that bind us: affordable healthcare, quality education, and economic opportunity for all. These issues impact people's lives, regardless of race, class, or background. When Democrats focus on policies that provide tangible benefits for everyone, they present a positive vision of the future that transcends narrow divides.

In contrast to MAGA's fear-driven rhetoric, which preys on insecurity and fuels cultural resentment, Democrats should offer a hopeful narrative grounded in practical solutions. This narrative should focus on healing and rebuilding, not merely reacting to the latest crisis or controversy. By framing their vision in terms of unity, opportunity, and shared prosperity, Democrats can win back the trust of those who feel alienated or overlooked by today's political discourse. The path forward lies not in catering to extremes, but in forging a middle ground that speaks to most Americans who seek stability, fairness, and a brighter future for their children.

While the MAGA movement has undoubtedly reshaped American politics, it has also created an opening for Democrats to offer a better path rooted in economic justice, social equality, and national unity. At a time when many Americans feel left behind by globalization, automation, and rising inequality, Democrats can advance policies that directly address the economic concerns of working-class voters while reaffirming their commitment to inclusion and civil rights. These goals are not mutually exclusive; they are deeply connected. Addressing financial and social inequality is essential to building a prosperous nation.

By standing firm on social justice—protecting the rights of women, LGBTQ+ individuals, and communities of color—while fighting for fair wages, affordable healthcare, and accessible education, Democrats can build a broad coalition of voters who believe in the promise of a better future. These policies should not be framed as benefiting one group at the expense of another, but as efforts that lift all Americans by fostering a more equitable and sustainable society. The nation benefits when everyone can access the opportunities that drive economic success and social mobility.

In the face of MAGA's politics of fear, Democrats must offer a vision that reflects the best of America's ideals—a nation that values democracy, fairness, and opportunity for all. This vision should celebrate diversity as a source of strength and emphasize that working together makes progress possible. The strength of America lies not in division but in unity, where our differences are embraced, and collective progress takes priority over political polarization.

By doing so, Democrats can build a more inclusive and equitable future that rises above division and embraces the power of collective action. This vision is about winning elections, restoring faith in democracy, and renewing hope for a better tomorrow. It is about reclaiming the national narrative from the forces of fear and offering a path forward that reflects the best of what America stands for: a country where everyone, regardless of background, can succeed and contribute to the common good.

Key takeaways

- To counter MAGA, Democrats must center their messaging on economic justice that benefits all Americans, not just identity-based appeals.

- Inclusive economic policies—like raising wages, expanding healthcare, and investing in infrastructure—can unite diverse communities.

- Social justice must be framed within a broader economic agenda to avoid alienating working-class voters and to build lasting coalitions.

- Policies like tax reform, labor rights, small business support, and criminal justice reform should be positioned as benefiting everyone, not just select groups.

- Democrats can reclaim ground by addressing economic frustrations MAGA exploits, while offering a forward-looking vision rooted in unity, fairness, and shared prosperity.

CHAPTER FOURTEEN

Fighting Misinformation and Engaging with MAGA Supporters

The rise of social media and the growing polarization of political discourse have created an environment where misinformation spreads rapidly, often drowning out facts and rational debate. The MAGA movement has proven particularly adept at exploiting this dynamic, using disinformation to reinforce its claims, deepen divisions, and rally its base around a distorted version of reality. However, the challenge goes beyond simply identifying falsehoods. Many MAGA supporters are not merely misled—they are deeply invested in an alternative political narrative that resonates with their emotions, frustrations, and lived experiences. Confronting misinformation, therefore, requires more than fact-checking; it demands understanding why so many people are drawn to these misleading narratives in the first place.

To effectively counter the MAGA narrative, Democrats must do more than debunk lies—they must engage constructively with individuals drawn to the movement by fear, resentment, and disillusionment. While it may be tempting to dismiss MAGA supporters as irrevocably lost to propaganda, doing so is both unfair and counterproductive. Many who align with the movement are not driven by ideological extremism, but by a sense of being unheard, overlooked, or betrayed by institutions that have failed to deliver on their promises. If Democrats hope to shift the political landscape, they must understand these grievances and offer an alternative vision that addresses the same anxieties, without relying on deception or division.

This chapter will explore strategies for combating misinformation, rebuilding trust in facts, and engaging with MAGA supporters in ways that promote meaningful political dialogue rather than further entrenching division. The goal is not to "win" arguments, but to plant seeds of doubt in false narratives, present credible and compelling alternatives, and show that Democratic policies can address the real concerns of many people who currently feel alienated from the party. It is a slow and often difficult process, but it is essential if America is to move beyond a cycle of reactionary politics fueled by disinformation.

The Role of Misinformation in MAGA's Success

Misinformation has played a crucial role in the rise and enduring influence of the MAGA movement. Unlike traditional political movements, MAGA has relied on a carefully constructed narrative, often rooted in false or misleading claims, to create a sense of urgency and division among its base. It is not merely a reaction to political policies or global events; it is a cultural and psychological campaign designed to rally people around a worldview in which Democrats and progressives are cast as existential threats. This narrative is reinforced daily, not just through speeches or rallies, but through a vast ecosystem of misinformation intended to sever MAGA supporters from credible sources of information.

A key tactic in this strategy is the relentless use of "fake news." Originally used to describe actual disinformation, the term has been co-opted and weaponized by MAGA figures to dismiss any news that contradicts their worldview. Whether it comes from reputable mainstream outlets or consists of factual reporting that challenges MAGA orthodoxy, labeling it "fake news" enables supporters to reject inconvenient truths without engaging with them. This tactic deepens confirmation bias and mistrust in institutions, reinforcing a sense of identity that sees MAGA as under siege by a hostile media and political elite.

The role of social media platforms and right-wing media in this process cannot be overstated. These channels serve as echo chambers, amplifying false claims and making it increasingly difficult for Americans, especially those in ideological bubbles, to distinguish fact from fiction. Algorithms designed to maximize engagement tend to elevate sensational or polarizing content, allowing misinformation to spread more widely and rapidly than accurate reporting. As a result, many MAGA supporters live in an alternate media reality where falsehoods are not only common but preferable, as they validate grievances and reinforce group identity.

This misinformation ecosystem has created an environment where rational discourse becomes nearly impossible. Facts alone cannot penetrate the armor of mistrust built through years of media manipulation and rhetorical conditioning. For Democrats, the challenge is twofold: they must combat specific falsehoods while confronting the broader culture of misinformation that has normalized disinformation as a political strategy. Meeting this challenge will require persistent public education, more substantial media literacy initiatives, and structural reforms to how online platforms operate.

The Big Lie and Election Fraud Claims

The "Big Lie"—the false claim that the 2020 presidential election was rigged—remains one of the most dangerous and enduring elements of the MAGA movement. Despite overwhelming evidence and dozens of court rulings affirming the election's integrity, Donald Trump and his allies have relentlessly promoted this falsehood to sow doubt about the legitimacy of the democratic process. What began as a baseless claim of voter fraud has metastasized into a full-blown conspiracy theory threatening the foundation of American democracy.

The damage caused by this lie cannot be overstated. Millions of Americans now believe—without evidence—that the 2020 election was stolen. This belief has eroded trust in electoral institutions, fueled political extremism, and led to tangible consequences, from the January 6th insurrection to the widespread harassment of election workers. Most significantly, the Big Lie has been used to justify a wave of state-level legislation restricting voting access. In the years following the 2020 election, hundreds of bills were introduced—and many passed—that imposed strict ID requirements, limited mail-in voting, purged voter rolls, or gave partisan officials greater control over election outcomes. These policies, all rooted in a false narrative, threaten to disenfranchise millions, particularly people of color, young voters, and those in urban communities.

For Democrats, responding to the Big Lie requires more than fact-checking—it demands a long-term commitment to restoring public confidence in the electoral system. This includes supporting federal legislation to protect voting rights, defending election officials who uphold the law, and increasing transparency in election processes. It also means holding accountable those who knowingly spread falsehoods for political gain, whether through legal channels or public condemnation. Only by affirming the legitimacy of democratic institutions can we begin to repair the damage done by a lie that refuses to die.

Conspiracy Theories and Fearmongering

Beyond the Big Lie, the MAGA movement thrives on a web of conspiracy theories that tap into deep-seated fears and insecurities. From the claim that COVID-19 was a government hoax, to accusations that Democrats are plotting to impose socialism, to the fringe belief in a global cabal of liberal elites—these narratives are not random. They are deliberately constructed to provoke fear, sow distrust, and cultivate tribal loyalty.

By portraying Democrats as members of a shadowy elite intent on destroying traditional American values, these conspiracy theories create a simplistic, emotionally charged "us vs. them" dynamic. In this worldview, MAGA supporters see themselves as patriots defending liberty, while opponents are framed as existential threats. This framing offers straightforward answers to complex problems. Rather than engage in nuanced debates on healthcare, immigration, or climate change, conspiracy theories supply scapegoats—often immigrants, minorities, or ideological "others."

The impact extends far beyond misinformation. These narratives have reshaped how many Americans engage with politics, replacing dialogue and debate with suspicion and hostility. Take, for example, the persistent myth that undocumented immigrants are driving up crime rates. Despite extensive evidence disproving this claim, the narrative persists because it aligns with broader cultural and demographic fear themes. These stories fuel resentment and reinforce policies that punish marginalized communities rather than address root causes like economic inequality or decaying infrastructure.

Importantly, these fears are not conjured from thin air—they stem from genuine anxieties about economic insecurity, cultural shifts, and political disempowerment. MAGA leaders exploit these vulnerabilities, offering emotional validation rather than practical solutions. Even when MAGA policies fail to deliver material gains, the movement's emotional resonance—its ability to name enemies and assign blame—keeps its base engaged.

For Democrats, the way forward is not to dismiss these fears as irrational, but to understand their origins and respond with empathy and substance. That means addressing economic dislocation, investing in underserved communities, and presenting a hopeful, inclusive vision for the future. It also means confronting misinformation with facts, building trust, and showing that progressive policies offer honest answers to people's challenges.

Fighting Misinformation: Restoring Trust in Facts

To reclaim the narrative and effectively counter the MAGA movement, Democrats must prioritize combating misinformation in ways that go beyond simply debunking false claims. Misinformation is not just about individual lies—it stems from a broader system of distorted narratives that have deeply embedded themselves in political discourse. Reinforced by years of partisan media, social media algorithms, and polarizing rhetoric, these narratives have reshaped how millions of Americans perceive truth and authority. To push back against MAGA falsehoods, Democrats must work to restore public trust in credible institutions—mainstream journalism, public education, scientific consensus, and nonpartisan government agencies—so that facts can once again play a central role in public debate.

Many MAGA supporters no longer trust traditional sources of information—not necessarily because of the reporting itself, but because years of disinformation have painted these outlets as irredeemably biased or hostile to conservative values. It is fair to acknowledge that outlets like The New York Times, CNN, or NPR may reflect specific editorial perspectives, and a healthy skepticism of media narratives is not inherently harmful. The problem arises when that skepticism becomes blanket distrust of the media and critical public institutions like the CDC, FBI, or Department of Justice. While imperfect, these agencies are essential in maintaining public health, national security, and the rule of law. Framing them as components of a "deep state" conspiracy erodes public trust and undermines a democratic society's ability to respond to crises with facts and expertise.

Restoring confidence in these institutions is not about denying bias but distinguishing between opinion-driven journalism and fact-based public service. Building trust is vital to defending democracy and restoring a shared sense of reality.

This transformation will not happen overnight or be achieved by Democrats alone. However, Democrats can lead by modeling transparency, promoting media literacy, and building relationships in communities that feel ignored or alienated by elite institutions. Rather than writing off MAGA supporters as lost causes, Democrats should engage with independents, moderates, and the "soft" MAGA base—those who may be skeptical of traditional media but are still open to respectful dialogue. Trust begins to rebuild when people feel heard, respected, and empowered, not dismissed or talked down to.

Breaking the echo chambers that MAGA supporters inhabit requires both digital and cultural strategies. Digitally, Democrats must support reforms that increase algorithmic transparency on social media and reduce the monetization of outrage-based content. They should also invest in alternative media and local journalism that reaches people where they are—via podcasts, YouTube channels, community newsletters, and trusted messengers. Faith leaders, veterans, small business owners, and even former MAGA figures can serve as effective, authentic voices for sharing factual information in a nonpartisan tone.

Culturally, Democrats must create space for people to question misinformation without fear of shame or ridicule. Fact-checking—while valuable—is often ineffective when delivered with condescension. Efforts to correct falsehoods should be grounded in empathy and shared values, connecting with what people care about: protecting their families, strengthening their communities, and building a better future for their children.

Ultimately, the goal is not to win every argument or convert every MAGA voter. It is to rebuild a political culture where truth matters and critical thinking is prioritized over ideological purity. That begins with making facts accessible, contextual, and emotionally resonant. Democrats must lead this cultural shift by embracing honesty, humility, and a long-term commitment to truth, even when it is politically inconvenient. Only then can we begin to repair the fractured information ecosystem that has allowed MAGA misinformation to flourish.

Promoting Media Literacy and Critical Thinking

One of the most potent tools Democrats have in the fight against misinformation is education. In an age where social media platforms have become central to how many Americans consume news, media literacy is no longer a luxury but a necessity. Platforms like Facebook, Instagram, X (formerly Twitter), and various podcast networks often function more as emotion engines than as sources of credible journalism. These spaces reward sensationalism, controversy, and emotionally charged content designed to drive engagement rather than accuracy. As a result, users are frequently exposed to material that reinforces their preexisting beliefs and biases, while discouraging thoughtful reflection or exposure to diverse perspectives.

The danger lies in the growing trend of people treating content from social media influencers, partisan podcasts, or unverified meme pages as equivalent—or even superior—to traditional journalism or peer-reviewed research. While these platforms can provide value when used responsibly, they are not substitutes for rigorous reporting or fact-based analysis. Algorithms prioritize content that generates outrage, often regardless of accuracy, enabling the viral spread of misleading narratives. When misinformation is consumed casually—as a meme, a viral tweet, or a provocative podcast soundbite—it bypasses critical scrutiny and becomes embedded in the broader political consciousness.

To combat this, Democrats should prioritize and invest in initiatives that promote media literacy at all levels of society. Media literacy is not just about spotting fake news—it involves understanding how information is constructed, how algorithms influence what we see, and how to evaluate the credibility of sources. Teaching people to distinguish factual reporting from opinion, identify confirmation bias, and recognize emotionally manipulative content is essential for building resilience against misinformation.

This educational effort should begin in schools, where students can be taught to navigate the digital information landscape responsibly. However, it must also extend to adults through community programs, public service campaigns, and partnerships with educational institutions and nonprofit organizations. Libraries, local news outlets, and bipartisan civic organizations can all play a role in fostering critical thinking skills across generations.

Promoting media literacy also means encouraging Americans to diversify their news consumption. Rather than relying solely on social media or ideologically aligned sources, people should be exposed to various perspectives, including those they may disagree with. Reintroducing citizens to trusted journalism—while acknowledging its limitations—can begin to repair the fractured information environment that has enabled MAGA misinformation to flourish.

Strengthening Fact-Checking and Independent Journalism

Fact-checking organizations are critical in debunking false claims and holding politicians and media figures accountable. Outlets like PolitiFact, FactCheck.org, and The Washington Post's Fact Checker provide an essential public service by scrutinizing political statements and exposing deliberate misinformation. However, their effectiveness depends heavily on public trust. In a political climate where many voters, especially those influenced by the MAGA movement, question the credibility of any institution that contradicts their worldview, even the most rigorous fact-checking can be dismissed as biased or conspiratorial.

Democrats must champion fact-checking not as a partisan weapon but as a fundamental safeguard of democratic accountability. This means advocating for public funding of independent journalism initiatives while ensuring these organizations maintain editorial independence. It also requires elevating local journalism, which has been severely underfunded in recent decades, leaving many communities more susceptible to misinformation. Local journalists, who often enjoy higher trust in their communities, are well-positioned to rebuild credibility in ways distant national outlets cannot.

Still, fact-checking alone is not enough. Misinformation thrives in digital environments where content spreads rapidly and without context. Social media platforms—Facebook, Instagram, YouTube, TikTok, and X (formerly Twitter)—play an outsized role in this ecosystem. These platforms prioritize engagement over accuracy, often amplifying the most provocative content regardless of its truthfulness. Democrats must demand greater accountability from tech companies by pushing for regulations that promote transparency in content moderation, algorithm design, and advertising policies. This includes urging platforms to more prominently feature verified information, flag misleading content, and reduce amplification of sources consistently identified as unreliable.

Engaging with MAGA Supporters: Moving Beyond the Divide

While debunking misinformation is necessary, it often fails to address MAGA loyalty's emotional and cultural drivers. Many supporters of the movement are not simply misinformed—they are angry, disillusioned, and searching for meaning in a rapidly changing world. To reach them, Democrats must move beyond presenting cold facts and speak to the political identity's emotional and personal aspects. This requires respect, not condescension—of engagement, not dismissal.

Meaningful dialogue starts by asking questions, not delivering lectures. Why do certain narratives resonate so profoundly with people? What unmet needs or fears fuel these beliefs? Democrats should approach each conversation as an opportunity to listen to understand concerns about job security, community decline, or cultural displacement. These anxieties are not irrational, and dismissing them outright only reinforces the MAGA narrative that Democrats are out of touch with "real America."

Furthermore, engagement must extend beyond political contexts. Faith groups, veterans' organizations, union halls, and town meetings are all spaces where authentic conversations can begin. Democrats should be present not just during election season but consistently, not to preach but to build genuine relationships.

Listening to Understand, Not to Argue

One of the most powerful yet underused tools in political engagement is genuine listening. When people feel genuinely heard and understood, they are far more likely to listen in return. It fosters mutual respect and opens the door to meaningful dialogue. For Democrats, active listening is an essential skill. This means creating an environment where individuals feel safe expressing their concerns, fears, and frustrations, without the immediate pressure of correction or rebuttal. Too often, the instinct is to counter arguments quickly, which can shut down productive conversations before they begin.

In many cases, MAGA supporters express concerns rooted in real, tangible fears, even if the conclusions they draw are flawed or misdirected. For example, economic decline in rural communities is a genuine issue affecting many working-class Americans' livelihoods. However, instead of acknowledging this struggle, some may falsely blame immigrants, global elites, or other scapegoats. While these conclusions are often misleading, the underlying fears—job loss, economic insecurity, and social displacement—deserve attention and empathy. Dismissing these concerns outright risks alienating voters who might otherwise be open to progressive solutions.

Instead, Democrats can engage constructively by offering accurate, practical solutions that directly address these communities' economic challenges. For instance, investing in green energy infrastructure in coal-dependent regions could create new jobs while helping to combat climate change. Expanding broadband access to rural areas would support local businesses and improve access to education, healthcare, and essential services. Apprenticeship programs that lead to well-paying, skilled jobs can provide an alternative path for those left behind by traditional education systems or a shifting labor market.

When people feel that Democrats understand their struggles and are committed to delivering concrete solutions, they become more open to reconsidering their views and exploring new ideas. This kind of engagement fosters collaboration and signals that Democrats are not merely seeking to win ideological battles but are genuinely invested in improving lives, especially for those who feel neglected by the political establishment.

Moreover, this approach can help dismantle the sense of alienation that MAGA rhetoric often exploits. By presenting an inclusive vision where everyone has a stake in a shared future, rather than portraying individuals as victims of a hostile elite, Democrats can begin to rebuild trust from the ground up. Instead of focusing solely on divisive arguments, they can promote a shared purpose that transcends party lines, showing that unity and progress are possible through empathy, understanding, and collective action.

Offering a Unifying Vision

Beyond addressing immediate concerns, Democrats must present a forward-looking vision that brings Americans together around shared values. While MAGA rhetoric thrives on division and fear, Democrats have the opportunity to offer a message that rises above those divisions. A unifying narrative should emphasize values most Americans agree on—freedom, fairness, opportunity, and justice. This is not about erasing differences, but embracing them as sources of strength. By focusing on the common good and highlighting America's diversity as one of its greatest assets, Democrats can present an inclusive future that appeals across the political spectrum.

A compelling unifying vision can be built around the following pillars:

1. **Economic Justice for All:** Democrats must champion policies that create well-paying jobs, expand access to affordable healthcare and housing, and reduce income inequality. These issues affect Americans across all demographics and can win support from progressives and conservatives frustrated by the widening wealth gap. When people experience tangible improvements in their lives—whether through better job opportunities, lower healthcare costs, or more accessible housing—they are more likely to embrace a message of shared prosperity and collective progress.

2. **Restoring Trust in Democracy:** Reaffirming the importance of voting rights, the rule of law, and an independent judiciary is critical when democratic institutions are under strain. Democrats must stand firmly to protect election integrity and ensure every vote counts. This message resonates with voters across the political spectrum who are alarmed by the erosion of democratic norms and institutions.

3. **Shared Values of Compassion and Equality:** Policies that protect marginalized groups—whether immigrants, communities of color, or LGBTQ+ individuals—should be framed not just as progressive priorities, but as expressions of core American values. Pursuing fairness, justice, and compassion transcends partisanship; it reflects the principles that have always shaped the American ideal. By situating these efforts within a broader, unifying message of equality, Democrats can move beyond partisan divides and appeal to voters' more profound sense of moral and civic responsibility.

Leading by Example: Reclaiming the Narrative

Democrats must lead by example in the fight against misinformation and political polarization, setting the tone for a more informed, compassionate, and unified political discourse. Reclaiming the narrative requires more than debunking false claims—cultivating a culture grounded in understanding, empathy, and constructive dialogue. In contrast to the fear-based tactics of the MAGA movement, which thrives on division, suspicion, and distrust, Democrats have a powerful opportunity to present a message of hope: hope for a future where facts matter, opportunity is within reach, and every citizen feels empowered to shape the nation's course.

Central to this vision is the belief that truth and information should be accessible and trusted. In a profoundly polarized environment, it is not enough to challenge falsehoods—we must also equip people with the tools to recognize them. Media literacy must become a cornerstone of Democratic initiatives, empowering individuals to critically evaluate the sources and accuracy of the information they encounter. Supporting independent journalism is equally vital, as a free and trustworthy press forms the foundation of any healthy democracy. Democrats can champion policies that elevate diverse, credible voices, helping to break through the echo chambers that fuel misinformation.

Still, addressing misinformation alone is not sufficient. Democrats must also offer a compelling, inclusive future vision that resonates with many Americans. That vision should center on the shared values of fairness, equality, and opportunity—principles that transcend partisanship and unite communities across cultural and political lines. It is not just about advocating for these values but delivering on them through policies that tangibly improve lives. Whether by creating economic opportunities, protecting social safety nets, or investing in infrastructure that benefits all Americans, Democrats must make clear that they are working to ensure everyone has a stake in the nation's future.

Engaging in respectful, fact-based dialogue can do more than counteract MAGA misinformation—it can begin to heal the divisions that define modern American politics. This engagement requires patience, empathy, and a willingness to hear the concerns of those who may genuinely disagree. Dismissing or belittling others only reinforces the divide. Instead, Democrats must model respectful discourse that rebuilds trust and fosters mutual respect. It will not happen overnight, but it is essential to the long-term health of our democracy.

Democrats also have the opportunity to reframe the national conversation around collective progress instead of cultural conflict. Rather than fighting battles that deepen polarization, they can elevate the common goals that unite Americans: the pursuit of fairness, the belief in opportunity, and the shared hope for a better future for the next generation. By emphasizing these unifying themes, Democrats can offer an alternative to the fear-driven rhetoric that MAGA perpetuates.

This vision, rooted in hope, inclusion, and practical solutions, charts a path forward that not only counters the dangers of misinformation and division but also lays the groundwork for a more just and democratic society. Democrats must lead this charge by showing that the fight for truth and progress is not about defeating opponents but about coming together to build a nation where everyone has the opportunity to succeed and contribute.

This work may seem daunting in a challenging political climate, but it is far from impossible. By uplifting shared values, advancing media literacy, strengthening independent journalism, and promoting an inclusive, future-focused vision, Democrats can reclaim the narrative. This is how we move forward—not just to defend facts, but to create a country where all Americans can find common ground, mutual respect, and genuine hope for tomorrow.

Key takeaways

- The "Big Lie" about the 2020 election eroded trust in democracy, justified voter suppression laws, and contributed to the Capitol insurrection.

- MAGA's success lies in emotional storytelling and fear-based narratives, not just political ideology—making fact-based rebuttals alone insufficient.

- Engaging MAGA supporters requires empathy, respect, and listening to the real fears behind their beliefs, such as economic insecurity and social change.

- Democrats must build trust by promoting local journalism, media literacy, and clear, inclusive messaging that resonates emotionally and economically.

- Countering misinformation includes empowering credible messengers, reforming social media practices, and investing in independent journalism.

- A unifying vision focused on fairness, economic justice, and shared values like opportunity and democracy will rebuild trust and offer a hopeful alternative to division.

Conclusion

Moving Forward Together

The MAGA movement has undeniably reshaped America's political landscape, leaving a deep and lasting imprint on the national discourse. Its rise has been fueled by misinformation, fear, and a profound sense of disillusionment among Americans who feel left behind in a rapidly changing world. By distorting facts, scapegoating vulnerable communities, and capitalizing on cultural and economic anxieties, MAGA has successfully mobilized a significant portion of the electorate. However, while its success is rooted in division, it also presents an opportunity for Democrats to reclaim the narrative and offer a more inclusive, forward-looking vision for the country's future.

To move forward, Democrats must confront MAGA's divisive rhetoric directly. This is not just about rejecting false claims but about offering a compelling alternative that addresses many Americans' legitimate concerns. Understanding the fears and frustrations MAGA has exploited is not about validating misinformation, but about responding with empathy and meaningful solutions. In doing so, Democrats can reconnect with disillusioned working-class voters while maintaining the trust of progressive constituencies. At its heart, the Democratic vision must be about more than opposition; it must unite the country around shared values—fairness, justice, and opportunity—through practical, results-driven policies.

Reclaiming this narrative will not be easy and will not happen overnight. However, in an era of deepening polarization, it is essential to the future of American democracy. Democrats must remain grounded in the issues that shape everyday life—economic inequality, healthcare access, racial justice, climate change, and education—while also acknowledging and addressing the cultural anxieties that MAGA has so effectively tapped into. By advancing concrete policies that directly impact people's lives—raising wages, expanding healthcare, making education more accessible, and confronting the climate crisis—Democrats can demonstrate that they are the party of solutions, not just slogans. Rebuilding trust and restoring hope will come not from rhetoric alone, but from results.

Equally vital is the task of restoring confidence in democratic institutions. MAGA's influence has eroded trust in government, elections, and the media. To counter this, Democrats must lead efforts to strengthen the integrity and accessibility of these institutions. That includes combating misinformation while promoting media literacy nationwide—helping Americans critically evaluate information in a landscape increasingly dominated by distortion and manipulation. Restoring trust also requires engaging in good-faith dialogue with those who feel alienated from the political process, including those drawn to MAGA. By listening with empathy and responding with real solutions, Democrats can bridge divides and break through the walls of cynicism and resentment.

While MAGA thrives on fear and division, Democrats must prioritize unity, empathy, and inclusive engagement, ensuring that every voice is heard and valued in the political conversation. This approach requires acknowledging that Americans' challenges are complex, multifaceted, and deeply interconnected. It is not just about countering a political movement but about cultivating a culture where solutions are grounded in facts, compassion, and shared values. Democrats must be the party that not only listens but also acts decisively to confront the structural and economic inequalities that MAGA has exploited.

By remaining committed to the principles of democracy, inclusivity, and justice, Democrats have the opportunity to rise above MAGA's toxic rhetoric and help build a more united, equitable America. Ultimately, the challenge is not merely to defeat a movement—it is to offer a vision of America that inspires hope, earns trust, and mobilizes collective action for the common good. The work ahead is urgent and transformative, but it is anchored in the values that have always defined America at its best.

The future of the nation is not predetermined. Its trajectory will depend on leaders' willingness to rise above division and pursue a shared purpose. Democrats now have the opportunity not just to win elections, but to help heal the rifts that have frayed the fabric of American society. The task is great, but the stakes are even more significant. By reclaiming the narrative, embracing the power of truth, and presenting a bold, inclusive vision for the future, Democrats can help shape a brighter, more unified America.

The fight is not just about the next election, but defining the future. Together, we can move forward. Together, we can build the America we all deserve: a country that is united, just, and committed to shared prosperity for all.

Glossary of Key Political Terms and Acronyms

ACA (Affordable Care Act): Landmark healthcare reform law passed in 2010 under President Obama aimed to expand health insurance coverage and reduce healthcare costs. Frequently targeted by conservatives as government overreach.

Birtherism: A conspiracy theory falsely claiming that President Barack Obama was not born in the United States and thus ineligible to serve as president. Heavily promoted by Donald Trump prior to his candidacy.

CBP (Customs and Border Protection): A federal law enforcement agency under the Department of Homeland Security responsible for securing U.S. borders and facilitating legal international trade and travel.

CDO (Collateralized Debt Obligation): A complex financial product backed by a pool of loans and assets. Widely associated with the 2008 financial crisis due to its role in the subprime mortgage collapse.

DACA (Deferred Action for Childhood Arrivals): An Obama-era program that provides temporary protection from deportation to undocumented immigrants brought to the U.S. as children.

Deep State: A term used to suggest the existence of a secretive network of unelected government officials working against elected leaders, often tied to conspiracy theories.

Glass-Steagall Act: A New Deal-era law separating commercial and investment banking. Its repeal in 1999 is often cited as a contributor to the 2008 crash.

GOP (Grand Old Party): Another name for the Republican Party

Epistemic Closure: A concept where individuals are so immersed in an ideological echo chamber that they dismiss outside information, reinforcing their own beliefs without challenge.

JCPOA (Joint Comprehensive Plan of Action): Commonly known as the Iran Nuclear Deal, signed in 2015 and later abandoned by Trump. It aimed to limit Iran's nuclear capabilities in exchange for lifting economic sanctions.

MAGA ("Make America Great Again"): A political slogan and movement centered around Donald Trump. It expresses nostalgia for a perceived better past, often linked to nationalist and populist themes.

NAFTA (North American Free Trade Agreement): A 1994 agreement between the U.S., Canada, and Mexico that eliminated most tariffs and trade barriers. Trump criticizes it as detrimental to American workers.

Neoliberalism: An economic philosophy promoting free markets, deregulation, and privatization. Criticized in the text for increasing inequality and weakening the social safety net.

Populism: A political approach claiming to represent the common people against elites. MAGA is framed as a form of right-wing populism driven by cultural and economic resentment.

TARP (Troubled Asset Relief Program): A 2008 program designed to stabilize the financial system during the Great Recession by bailing out banks and automakers.

Tea Party: A conservative movement that emerged after the 2008 financial crisis, initially focused on reducing government spending and taxes, later morphing into a populist and anti-establishment force.

Title 42: A public health law used during the Trump and early Biden administrations to expel migrants at the border without asylum processing, citing COVID-19 concerns.

Title 8: The main section of U.S. immigration law dealing with enforcement and penalties for unauthorized immigration, reinstated after the expiration of Title 42.

TCJA (Tax Cuts and Jobs Act): A 2017 tax law passed under Trump that cut corporate tax rates and adjusted individual tax brackets. Criticized for disproportionately benefiting the wealthy.

WTO (World Trade Organization): An international organization that regulates trade between nations. China's 2001 entry into the WTO is a major factor in U.S. manufacturing job losses.

Wokeism: A term used, often pejoratively, to describe progressive awareness of social justice issues. MAGA figures frequently critique it as excessive political correctness.

Southern Strategy: A Republican strategy from the 1960s-70s that used coded racial language to gain support among white voters disaffected by civil rights gains.

References

PART 1: THE RISE OF MAGA

Chapter 1: The Political and Economic Roots of MAGA

Acemoglu, D., & Restrepo, P. (2020). *Robots and jobs: Evidence from US labor markets. Journal of Political Economy, 128*(6), 2188-2244. Retrieved from https://doi.org/10.1086/705716

Autor, D. H., Dorn, D., & Hanson, G. H. (2016). *The China shock: Learning from labor-market adjustment to large changes in trade. Annual Review of Economics, 8*(1), 205-240. Retrieved from https://doi.org/10.1146/annurev-economics-080315-015041

Bureau of Labor Statistics. (2021). *Employment, hours, and earnings from the Current Employment Statistics survey (National)*. U.S. Department of Labor. Retrieved from https://www.bls.gov/ces/

Bown, C. P. (2020). *US-China phase one tracker: China's purchases of US goods.* Peterson Institute for International Economics. Retrieved from https://www.piie.com/research/piie-charts/us-china-phase-one-tracker-chinas-purchases-us-goods

Case, A., & Deaton, A. (2020). *Deaths of despair and the future of capitalism.* Princeton University Press.

Federal Reserve Bank of St. Louis. (n.d.). *All employees, manufacturing (MANEMP) [Data set].* FRED Economic Data. Retrieved from https://fred.stlouisfed.org/series/MANEMP#

Granlund, D. (2010, September 19). Tea Party vs. GOP [Cartoon]. Hannibal Courier-Post. Retrieved from https://www.hannibal.net/archive/article/granlund-cartoon-tea-party-vs-gop/article_1f85a8b5-5a18-5687-b9a0-b563434f6106.html

Hofstadter, R. (1964). *The paranoid style in American politics and other essays*. Harvard University Press.

Leonhardt, D. (2021, November 23). Working-class white Americans are now dying in middle age at faster rates than minority groups. Brookings Institution. Retrieved from https://www.brookings.edu/articles/working-class-white-americans-are-now-dying-in-middle-age-at-faster-rates-than-minority-groups/

Sen, A., & Cutler, D. M. (2023). Blue laws, religious observance, and health outcomes. National Bureau of Economic Research. Retrieved from https://www.nber.org/bh/20232/blue-laws-religious-observance-and-health-outcomes

Skocpol, T., & Williamson, V. (2016). *The Tea Party and the remaking of Republican conservatism*. Oxford University Press.

Skowronek, S. (2011). *Presidential leadership in political time: Reprise and reappraisal*. University Press of Kansas.

World Trade Organization. (2001). *Ministerial declaration*. Retrieved from

Chapter 2: The Tea Party and the Prelude to Trump

CBS News. (2010, April 14). CBS News/New York Times poll: Tea Party movement. CBS News. Retrieved from https://www.cbsnews.com/news/cbs-newsnew-york-times-poll-tea-party-movement/

Congressional Budget Office. (2012). Report on the Troubled Asset Relief Program (TARP). Retrieved from https://www.cbo.gov/publication/42921

Feldman, S. (2014). Racial resentment and the Tea Party. Political Psychology, 35(4), 469-478. Retrieved from https://doi.org/10.1111/pops.12084

Knowles, E. D., Lowery, B. S., & Schaumberg, R. L. (2010). Racial prejudice predicts opposition to Obama and his healthcare reform plan. Journal of Experimental Social Psychology, 46(2), 420-423. Retrieved from https://doi.org/10.1016/j.jesp.2009.10.011

Mian, A., & Sufi, A. (2014). House of debt: How they (and you) caused the Great Recession, and how we can prevent it from happening again. University of Chicago Press.

Parker, C. S., & Barreto, M. A. (2013). Change they can't believe in: The Tea Party and reactionary politics in America. Princeton University Press.

Pew Research Center. (2011). Birtherism persists among Tea Party Republicans. Retrieved from https://www.pewresearch.org/fact-tank/2011/04/21/birtherism-persists-among-tea-party-republicans/

Pew Research Center. (2011, May 4). Obama 2012 and the Tea Party. Retrieved from https://www.pewresearch.org/politics/2011/05/04/section-6-obama-2012-and-the-tea-party/#b76879129a6b53218285849e18bae77e

Santelli, R. (2009, February 19). Rick Santelli's Tea Party rant [Video]. CNBC. Retrieved from https://www.cnbc.com/video/2009/02/19/cnbc-video-of-rick-santellis-tea-party-rant.html

Skocpol, T., & Williamson, V. (2016). The Tea Party and the remaking of Republican conservatism. Oxford University Press.

Tesler, M. (2016). Post-racial or most-racial? Race and politics in the Obama era. University of Chicago Press.

Chapter 3: Trump's Political Ascent

Boczkowski, P. J., Mitchelstein, E., & Matassi, M. (2018). Trump, the media, and the debate over post-truth politics. International Journal of Communication, 12, 3550–3569.

Cramer, K. J. (2016). The politics of resentment: Rural consciousness in Wisconsin and the rise of Scott Walker. University of Chicago Press.

Fraser, S. (2015). The age of acquiescence: The life and death of American resistance to organized wealth and power. Little, Brown and Company.

Gillion, D. Q. (2020). The loud minority: Why protests matter in American democracy. Princeton University Press.

Heer, J. (2019). What Trump understood about America. The New Republic. Retrieved from https://newrepublic.com/article/153459/trump-understood-america

Hemmer, N. (2019). Messengers of the right: Conservative media and the transformation of American politics. University of Pennsylvania Press.

Hooghe, M., & Dassonneville, R. (2018). Explaining the Trump vote: The effect of racist resentment and anti-immigrant sentiments. PS: Political Science & Politics, 51(3), 528–534. Retrieved from https://doi.org/10.1017/S1049096518000367

Jardina, A. (2019). White identity politics. Cambridge University Press.

Levitsky, S., & Ziblatt, D. (2018). How democracies die. Crown Publishing Group.

McAdam, D., & Kloos, K. (2019). Deeply divided: Racial politics and social movements in postwar America. Oxford University Press.

Ott, B. L. (2017). The age of Twitter: Donald J. Trump and the politics of debasement. Critical Studies in Media Communication, 34(1), 59-68. Retrieved from https://doi.org/10.1080/15295036.2016.1266686

Sides, J., Tesler, M., & Vavreck, L. (2018). Identity crisis: The 2016 presidential campaign and the battle for the meaning of America. Princeton University Press.

PART 2: THE RHETORIC OF MAGA—APPEAL VS. REALITY

Chapter 4: "Make America Great Again" – A Nostalgic Myth?

Coontz, S. (2011). A strange stirring: The Feminine Mystique and American women at the dawn of the 1960s. Basic Books.

Cowie, J. (2010). Stayin' alive: The 1970s and the last days of the working class. New Press.

Dovere, E. I. (2016). Trump's nostalgia trap. Politico Magazine. https://www.politico.com/magazine/story/2016/05/donald-trump-2016-nostalgia-213909/

Federal Bureau of Investigation. (2021). Crime in the United States. https://www.fbi.gov/services/cjis/ucr

Gitlin, T. (1987). The sixties: Years of hope, days of rage. Bantam Books.

Hochschild, A. R. (2016). Strangers in their own land: Anger and mourning on the American right. New Press.

Johnson, D. K. (2004). The Lavender Scare: The Cold War persecution of gays and lesbians in the federal government. University of Chicago Press.

Katznelson, I. (2005). When affirmative action was white: An untold history of racial inequality in twentieth-century America. W.W. Norton & Company.

Norris, P., & Inglehart, R. (2019). Cultural backlash: Trump, Brexit, and authoritarian populism. Cambridge University Press.

Parks, W. R. (1997). *The McCarthy era and its impact on American politics*. University Press.

Piketty, T. (2014). Capital in the twenty-first century. Harvard University Press.

Rothstein, R. (2017). *The color of law: A forgotten history of how our government segregated America.* Liveright Publishing.

Sides, J., Tesler, M., & Vavreck, L. (2018). *Identity crisis: The 2016 presidential campaign and the battle for the meaning of America.* Princeton University Press.

Statista. (n.d.). *United States unemployment number & rate historical.* Statista. Retrieved from https://www.statista.com/statistics/1315397/united-states-unemployment-number-rate-historical/

Taylor, K. (2019). *Race for profit: How banks and the real estate industry undermined Black homeownership.* University of North Carolina Press.

Urban Institute. (n.d.). *Nine charts about wealth inequality in America (updated).* Retrieved from https://apps.urban.org/features/wealth-inequality-charts/

Chapter 5: The "Deep State" and Distrust in Institutions

Benkler, Y., Faris, R., & Roberts, H. (2018). *Network propaganda: Manipulation, disinformation, and radicalization in American politics.* Oxford University Press.

Brennan Center for Justice. (2023). *Voting laws roundup: The surge in voter suppression laws continues.* https://www.brennancenter.org/our-work/research-reports/voting-laws-roundup-september-2024

Enten, H. (2023, August 5). The big reason Trump leads the GOP field: Republicans think he won in 2020. CNN. https://www.cnn.com/2023/08/05/politics/2020-election-predictor-2024/index.html

Gallup. (2023, November 3). Partisan split on election integrity gets even wider. Gallup. https://news.gallup.com/poll/651185/partisan-split-election-integrity-gets-even-wider.aspx

Gauchat, G. (2012). Politicization of science in the public sphere: A study of public trust in the United States, 1974 to 2010. American Sociological Review, 77(2), 167-187. Retrieved from https://doi.org/10.1177/0003122412438225

Goldenberg, S. L. (2021). Anti-government, anti-science: Why conservatives have turned against science. Dædalus, 150(3), 86-101. Retrieved from https://www.amacad.org/publication/daedalus/anti-government-anti-science-why-conservatives-have-turned-against-science

Gross, L. (2016). The secret lives of animals: How the study of animal behavior contributes to science. *Science & Society, 34*(5), 299-311.

Ipsos. (2021). A majority of Republicans still believe the 2020 election was stolen. Retrieved from https://www.ipsos.com/en-us/news-polls/republicans-believe-2020-election-was-stolen

Ipsos. (2021). Public trust in election integrity: Republican and Democrat perspectives. Retrieved from https://www.ipsos.com

Lewandowsky, S. (2021). The "infodemic": The role of conspiracy theories in the spread of COVID-19 misinformation. Journal of Applied Research in Memory and Cognition, 10(2), 164-173. Retrieved from https://doi.org/10.1016/j.jarmac.2021.04.001

Miller, C. (2020). Trump's deep state: The assault on American institutions. Brookings Institution Press.

O'Connor, C., & Weatherall, J. O. (2019). The misinformation age: How false beliefs spread. Yale University Press.

Rosenfeld, S. (2021). The stolen election myth and the rise of insurrectionist violence. Journal of Democracy, 32(4), 117-131. Retrieved from https://doi.org/10.1353/jod.2021.0067

Waddell, C. (2009, March 9). Caught on film: The treadmill-running shrimp that became an instant internet sensation. *Daily Mail*.

Waisbord, S. (2018). Truth is what happens to news: On journalism, fake news, and post-truth. Journalism Studies, 19(13), 1866-1878. Retrieved from https://doi.org/10.1080/1461670X.2018.1492881

Zimmer, C. (2011). A tale of a shrimp on a treadmill: The truth behind the viral science story. *Discover Magazine*. Retrieved from https://www.discovermagazine.com

Chapter 6: The "America First" Illusion

Amiti, M., Redding, S. J., & Weinstein, D. E. (2019). The impact of the 2018 tariffs on U.S. prices and welfare. Journal of Economic Perspectives, 33(4), 187-210. Retrieved from https://doi.org/10.1257/jep.33.4.187

Bertelsmann Stiftung. (n.d.). Did the Trans-Pacific Partnership deal (TPP) benefit the U.S.? Retrieved from https://www.bertelsmann-stiftung.de/en/publications/publication/did/the-trans-pacific-partnership-deal-tpp/

Bown, C. P. (2020). The WTO and the crisis in global trade. Brookings Institution Press.

Dickerson, C. (2021, February 22). Families still separated after Trump's "zero tolerance" policy. The New York Times. Retrieved from https://www.nytimes.com/2021/02/22/us/family-separation-zero tolerance.html

Habbach, D., Hampton, S., & Mishori, R. (2020). The impact of Trump's zero-tolerance policy on children at the border. American Journal of Public Health, 110(12), 1701-1705. Retrieved from https://doi.org/10.2105/AJPH.2020.305859

Jordan, M. (2019, August 8). Immigration raids leave Mississippi businesses struggling. The New York Times. Retrieved from https://www.nytimes.com/2019/08/08/us/immigration-raids-mississippi.html

Light, M. T., & Miller, T. (2018). Immigration and crime: The relationship between immigration and crime rates in the U.S. Criminal Justice Policy Review, 29(2), 201-223. Retrieved from https://doi.org/10.1177/0887403417722202

Ousey, G. C., & Kubrin, C. E. (2018). Immigration and crime: The effects of immigration on crime rates in U.S. metropolitan areas. Social Problems, 65(3), 347-364. Retrieved from https://doi.org/10.1093/socpro/spx035

Petri, P. A., & Plummer, M. G. (2016). The Trans-Pacific Partnership: The economic implications of the TPP for the U.S. and its partners. Asian Economic Policy Review, 11(2), 298-318. Retrieved from https://doi.org/10.1111/aepr.12148

National Academies of Sciences, Engineering, and Medicine. (2017). The economic and fiscal consequences of immigration. The National Academies Press. Retrieved from

Chapter 7: The Culture War as a Political Strategy

AACTE. (2021). *The role of teacher education in the 21st century*. AACTE. https://aacte.org

Brownstein, R. (2017). Trump's culture wars: How conservative media kept MAGA's base motivated. The Atlantic. Retrieved from https://www.theatlantic.com/politics/archive/2017/08/trumps-culture-wars/535871/

Delgado, R., & Stefancic, J. (2017). Critical race theory: An introduction (3rd ed.). New York University Press.

Ferguson, S. A. (2022). The weaponization of LGBTQ+ rights in the culture war. Journal of LGBTQ Issues in Counseling, 16(1), 44-59. Retrieved from https://doi.org/10.1080/15538605.2022.2042093

Gallup. (2021). *Americans' views on the teaching of race and LGBTQ+ issues in schools*. Gallup. https://www.gallup.com

Harris, R. (2020). The real priorities of parents in America. *Education Week*. https://www.edweek.org

Hartzog, W., & Stulberg, L. M. (2022). Woke capitalism: Corporate America's role in the culture war. Business and Society Review, 127(4), 475-493. Retrieved from https://doi.org/10.1111/basr.12230

Jenkins, P. (2021). Moral panics and political mobilization: The effectiveness of manufactured cultural crises in American politics. American Political Science Review, 115(2), 375-389. Retrieved from https://doi.org/10.1017/S0003055421000104

National Education Association. (2021). *Teachers' roles in addressing political and social issues in classrooms*. NEA. https://www.nea.org

Pew Research Center. (2022, October 27). Views of the U.S. as a Christian nation and opinions about Christian nationalism. Retrieved from https://www.pewresearch.org/religion/2022/10/27/views-of-the-u-s-as-a-christian-nation-and-opinions-about-christian-nationalism/pf_2022-10-27_christian-nationalism_3-01-png/

Sides, J., Tesler, M., & Vavreck, L. (2018). Identity crisis: The 2016 presidential campaign and the battle for the meaning of America. Princeton University Press.

Zhao, Y. (2017). *The power of diversity in education: Why engaging multiple perspectives makes us smarter*. Educational Researcher, 46(2), 91-98. https://doi.org/10.3102/0034654316675213

Whitehead, A. L., & Perry, S. L. (2020). Taking America back for God: Christian nationalism in the United States. Oxford University Press.

PART 3: DEBUNKING THE DECONTEXTUALIZED ARGUMENTS OF MAGA

Chapter 8: The Economy Under Trump vs. Biden

Bernstein, J. (2021). *Why the American Rescue Plan worked*. The Brookings Institution. https://www.brookings.edu/opinions/why-the-american-rescue-plan-worked/

Bittman, M. (2022, September 14). *The real reason food costs have skyrocketed*. The Bittman Project. https://bittmanproject.com/the-real-reason-food-costs-have-skyrocketed/

Bivens, J., & Mishel, L. (2019). The failure of tax cuts to boost wages for working people. Economic Policy Institute. Retrieved from https://www.epi.org

Blanchard, O. (2022). The impact of the American Rescue Plan on the U.S. economy: An overview. Peterson Institute for International Economics. Retrieved from https://www.piie.com

Bureau of Economic Analysis (BEA). (2020). Gross domestic product, fourth quarter and year 2019 (second estimate). U.S. Department of Commerce. https://www.bea.gov

Bureau of Labor Statistics (BLS). (2020). Employment, hours, and earnings from the Current Employment Statistics survey (National). U.S. Department of Labor. https://www.bls.gov

Bureau of Labor Statistics. (2022). *Employment situation summary, December 2021*. U.S. Department of Labor. https://www.bls.gov/news.release/empsit.nr0.htm

Bureau of Labor Statistics. (2023). The employment situation – January 2023. Bureau of Labor Statistics. Retrieved from https://www.bls.gov/news.release/pdf/empsit.pdf

Cava, M. (2023, January 31). *ExxonMobil smashes Western oil majors' earnings record with $56 billion profit*. Reuters. https://www.reuters.com/business/energy/exxon-smashes-western-oil-majors-earnings-record-with-56-billion-profit-2023-01-31/

Congressional Budget Office (CBO). (2019). The budget and economic outlook: 2019 to 2029. https://www.cbo.gov/publication/54918

Congressional Budget Office. (2020). An update to the budget outlook: 2020 to 2030. Retrieved from https://www.cbo.gov

Centers for Disease Control and Prevention. (2021). *COVID-19 vaccine distribution and funding overview*. https://www.cdc.gov/coronavirus/2019-ncov/vaccines/distribution.html

Dunkley, E. (2023, January 31). *Chevron posts record profits in 2022*. NPR. https://www.npr.org/2023/01/31/1152776315/exxon-mobil-earnings-chevron-big-oil-biden-windfall-tax

Federal Reserve. (2021). Economic data and analysis: Job creation and economic trends under Obama and Trump administrations. Retrieved from https://www.federalreserve.gov/

Federal Reserve. (2021). Unemployment rate trends, 2009-2020. Federal Reserve Economic Data (FRED). Federal Reserve Bank of St. Louis. https://fred.stlouisfed.org

Federal Reserve. (2022). *Monetary policy report – June 2022*. https://www.federalreserve.gov/monetarypolicy/mpr_default.htm

Federal Reserve Bank of St. Louis. (n.d.). All employees: Manufacturing [Data set]. FRED, Federal Reserve Economic Data. Retrieved from https://fred.stlouisfed.org/series/MANEMP

Federal Reserve Bank of St. Louis. (n.d.). Real gross domestic product (GDPC1) [Data set]. FRED, Federal Reserve Bank of St. Louis. Retrieved from https://fred.stlouisfed.org/series/GDPC1

International Monetary Fund. (2022). World economic outlook: Inflation and economic recovery. International Monetary Fund. Retrieved from https://www.imf.org/en/Publications/WEO

International Monetary Fund. (2022). *World economic outlook: War sets back the global recovery*. https://www.imf.org/en/Publications/WEO/Issues/2022/04/19/world-economic-outlook-april-2022

International Monetary Fund. (2023). Consumer price inflation trends in the U.S. and globally. International Monetary Fund DataMapper. Retrieved from https://www.imf.org/external/datamapper/PCPIPCH@WEO/WEOWORLD/USA

Konczal, M., & Lusiani, N. (2023). Corporate profiteering and inflation: How businesses capitalized on the pandemic. The Roosevelt Institute. Retrieved from https://www.rooseveltinstitute.org/

Krugman, P. (2021). *The case for stimulus: Why the risk of doing too little outweighed inflation concerns*. The New York Times. https://www.nytimes.com/2021/03/11/opinion/stimulus-inflation-biden.html

Mariani, C. (2022, July 13). *PepsiCo CFO anticipates continued price hikes due to inflation*. CFO Dive. https://www.cfodive.com/news/pepsico-cfo-anticipating-continued-price-hikes-due-to-inflation/607706/

Miller, A. (2023). Understanding the American Rescue Plan: A report on its economic impacts. Brookings Institution. Retrieved from https://www.brookings.edu/

Parolin, Z., Curran, M., Matsudaira, J., Waldfogel, J., & Wimer, C. (2021). *Monthly poverty rates in the United States during the COVID-19 pandemic*. Columbia University Center on Poverty and Social Policy. https://www.povertycenter.columbia.edu/news-internal/2021/covid-19-monthly-poverty-march-2021

Reuters. (2019). U.S. companies set record $1 trillion in stock buybacks in 2018. Retrieved from https://www.reuters.com

Stacker. (2023). What's behind the growing number of manufacturing jobs in the U.S.? Retrieved from https://stacker.com/business-economy/whats-behind-growing-number-manufacturing-jobs

Summers, L. (2021). *Opinion: The inflation risk of the American Rescue Plan*. The Washington Post. https://www.washingtonpost.com/opinions/larry-summers-inflation-risk-biden/

Tax Policy Center. (2018). The distributional effects of the 2017 tax cuts. Urban-Brookings Tax Policy Center. Retrieved from https://www.taxpolicycenter.org/

U.S. Congress. (2021). *American Rescue Plan Act of 2021*. Public Law No. 117-2. https://www.congress.gov/bill/117th-congress/house-bill/1319

White House. (2021). Fact sheet: The Bipartisan Infrastructure Law's impact on the economy. Retrieved from https://www.whitehouse.gov/briefing-room/statements-releases/2021/11/15/fact-sheet-bipartisan-infrastructure-law/

Zucman, G., & Saez, E. (2020). The triumph of injustice: How the rich dodge taxes and how to make them pay. W.W. Norton & Company.

Zucman, G., & Saez, E. (2020). The role of tax policy in economic inequality and corporate taxation under Trump. Journal of Economic Perspectives, 34(2), 109-126. https://doi.org/10.1257/jep.34.2.109

Chapter 9: Immigration—Facts vs. Fear

American Immigration Council. (2019). Deportation and due process: How U.S. immigration policies affect undocumented immigrants. Retrieved from https://www.americanimmigrationcouncil.org

American Immigration Council. (2023). Title 42 and its impact on immigration enforcement. Retrieved from https://www.americanimmigrationcouncil.org

Card, D. (2009). Immigration and inequality. American Economic Review, 99(2), 1-21. Retrieved from https://doi.org/10.1257/aer.99.2.1

CBP. (2023). Southwest border encounters FY 2022. U.S. Customs and Border Protection. Retrieved from https://www.cbp.gov/newsroom/stats/southwest-land-border-encounters

Census Bureau. (2023). Age and sex pyramid for the United States: Population trends. U.S. Census Bureau. Retrieved from https://www.census.gov/library/visualizations/interactive/age-sex-pyramid-for-the-united-states.html

Krogstad, J. M. (2023). Biden's immigration policies: Enforcement and legal pathways. Pew Research Center. Retrieved from https://www.pewresearch.org/fact-tank/2023/04/12/biden-immigration-policies/

National Academy of Sciences. (2017). The economic and fiscal consequences of immigration. National Academies Press. Retrieved from https://doi.org/10.17226/23550

Nowrasteh, A. (2020). The impact of Trump's immigration policies on deportations and enforcement. Cato Institute. Retrieved from https://www.cato.org/publications

Orrenius, P. M., & Zavodny, M. (2019). Do immigrants compete with native-born workers? National Bureau of Economic Research. Retrieved from https://doi.org/10.3386/w23032

Peri, G. (2020). The economic impact of immigration: Productivity, employment, and wages. Journal of Economic Perspectives, 34(4), 133-156. Retrieved from https://doi.org/10.1257/jep.34.4.133

Pew Research Center. (2021). U.S. immigration enforcement statistics: A historical perspective. Retrieved from https://www.pewresearch.org/fact-tank/2021/08/20/u-s-immigration-enforcement-trends/

Rosenblum, M. R., & Meissner, D. (2014). The deportation dilemma: Reconciling tough and humane enforcement. Migration Policy Institute. Retrieved from https://www.migrationpolicy.org/research/deportation-dilemma-reconciling-tough-humane-enforcement

Statista. (2023). Global net per capita migration by country. Retrieved from https://www.statista.com/chart/28351/global-net-per-capita-migration-by-country/

United Nations. (2022). Global migration trends: Drivers and patterns of movement. United Nations Department of Economic and Social Affairs. Retrieved from https://www.un.org/en/development/desa/population/migration/data

U.S. Department of Homeland Security. (2022). Yearbook of Immigration Statistics, 2022. Retrieved from https://ohss.dhs.gov/topics/immigration/yearbook/2022

Chapter 10: Law and Order – Crime, Protests, and Policing

Brennan Center for Justice. (2023). FBI data confirms drop in most crimes in 2023, especially murders. Retrieved from https://www.brennancenter.org/our-work/analysis-opinion/fbi-data-confirms-drop-most-crimes-2023-especially-murders

Bureau of Justice Statistics. (2023). *Crime trends in the United States*. U.S. Department of Justice. https://www.bjs.gov

Chicago Police Department. (2023). *Annual crime report 2023*. https://home.chicagopolice.org

Cook, P. J., & Goss, K. A. (2020). *The gun debate: What everyone needs to know*. Oxford University Press.

FBI. (2021). Crime in the United States: 2020 Uniform Crime Report. Federal Bureau of Investigation. Retrieved from https://ucr.fbi.gov/crime-in-the-u.s/2020

FBI. (2023). Crime statistics for 2023: National crime trends and analysis. Federal Bureau of Investigation. Retrieved from https://www.fbi.gov/services/cjis/ucr

Federal Bureau of Investigation. (2023). *Crime in the United States, 2023*. U.S. Department of Justice. https://www.fbi.gov

Los Angeles Police Department. (2023). *Crime data and statistics 2023*. https://www.lapdonline.org

Maguire, E. R., Nix, J., & Campbell, B. A. (2021). A war on cops? The effects of Ferguson on the number of U.S. police officers murdered in the line of duty. Justice Quarterly, 38(1), 1-23. Retrieved from https://doi.org/10.1080/07418825.2020.1789699

New York Police Department. (2023). *NYPD crime statistics: Mid-year report 2023*. https://www.nyc.gov/nypd

Pew Research Center. (2023). Crime and safety in American cities: Public perception versus reality. Retrieved from https://www.pewresearch.org/social-trends/2023/

Ray, R. (2020). What does "defund the police" mean and does it have merit? Brookings Institution. Retrieved from https://www.brookings.edu/articles/what-does-defund-the-police-mean-and-does-it-have-merit/

Rosenfeld, R., Abt, T., & Lopez, E. (2021). Pandemic, social unrest, and crime in U.S. cities. Council on Criminal Justice. Retrieved from https://counciloncj.org/pandemic-social-unrest-and-crime-in-u-s-cities/

Siegel, M., Ross, C. S., & King, C. (2013). The relationship between gun ownership and firearm homicide rates in the United States, 1981–2010. *American Journal of Public Health, 103*(11), 2098–2105. https://doi.org/10.2105/AJPH.2013.301409

Small Arms Survey. (2021). *Estimating global civilian-held firearms numbers*. Graduate Institute of International and Development Studies. Retrieved from https://smallarmssurvey.org

Small Arms Survey. (2021). U.S. firearm sales and violence trends during COVID-19. Retrieved from https://www.smallarmssurvey.org/resource/us-firearm-sales-and-violence-trends-during-covid-19

Urban Institute. (2023). Public safety funding trends: Have cities defunded the police? Retrieved from https://www.urban.org/research/public-safety-funding-trends

White House. (2022). Bipartisan Safer Communities Act: Investing in community safety and law enforcement. Retrieved from https://www.whitehouse.gov/briefing-room/statements-releases/2022/06/25/bipartisan-safer-communities-act/

Chapter 11: Election Fraud and the Big Lie

Brookings Institution. (n.d.). How widespread is election fraud in the United States? Not very. Retrieved from https://www.brookings.edu/articles/how-widespread-is-election-fraud-in-the-united-states-not-very/

Brennan Center for Justice. (2021). Voting laws roundup: The continued push for voter suppression. Retrieved from https://www.brennancenter.org/our-work/research-reports/voting-laws-roundup

Dominion Voting Systems v. Fox News Network, LLC, No. N21C-03-257 EMD (Del. Super. Ct. 2023).

Federal Bureau of Investigation. (2021). FBI statement on the January 6th attack on the U.S. Capitol. Retrieved from https://www.fbi.gov/news/pressrel/press-releases/fbi-statement-on-the-january-6-attack

Ideastream Public Media. (2024, October 3). Driven by Republicans, most Americans are concerned about fraud in the 2024 election. Retrieved from https://www.ideastream.org/npr-news/2024-10-03/driven-by-republicans-most-americans-are-concerned-about-fraud-in-the-2024-election

Ipsos. (2021). Majority of Republicans still believe the 2020 election was stolen, poll finds. Retrieved from https://www.ipsos.com/en-us/news-polls/republican-belief-2020-election-stolen

PolitiFact. (2020). Fact-checking claims of election fraud in the 2020 presidential election. Retrieved from https://www.politifact.com/factchecks/2020

Rosenfeld, S. (2021). Why do so many Americans still believe the Big Lie?. The Guardian. Retrieved from https://www.theguardian.com/us-news/2021/dec/23/why-americans-still-believe-trump-big-lie

Trump v. Boockvar, No. 20-3371 (3rd Cir. 2020).

Trump, D. J. (2021, January 6). Speech at the "Save America" rally. Washington, D.C.

United States Department of Justice. (2020). Attorney General William Barr: No evidence of widespread voter fraud in 2020 election. Retrieved from https://www.justice.gov/opa/pr/ag-barr-no-evidence-election-fraud

White House. (2021). Statement by President Biden on the January 6th attack on democracy. Retrieved from https://www.whitehouse.gov/briefing-room/statements-releases/2021/01/06/president-biden-statement-on-january-6-attack

Chapter 12: Foreign Policy—The Myth of Trump's "Peace Presidency"

Belfer Center for Science and International Affairs. (2020). *Impacts of the U.S. Killing of Qassem Soleimani*. Retrieved from https://www.belfercenter.org/publication/impacts-us-killing-qassem-soleimani

Bown, C. P. (2020). *The US-China trade war and phase one agreement*. Peterson Institute for International Economics. Retrieved from https://www.piie.com/publications/policy-briefs/us-china-trade-war-and-phase-one-agreement

Bureau of Investigative Journalism. (2017). *Drone wars: the full data*. Retrieved from https://www.thebureauinvestigates.com/stories/2017-01-01/drone-wars-the-full-data/

Bureau of Investigative Journalism. (2017). *US counter terror air strikes double in Trump's first year*. Retrieved from https://www.thebureauinvestigates.com/stories/2017-12-19/counterrorism-strikes-double-trump-first-year/

Chicago Sun-Times. (2019). *Under Donald Trump, drone strikes far exceed Obama's numbers*. Retrieved from https://chicago.suntimes.com/news/2019/5/8/18619206/under-donald-trump-drone-strikes-far-exceed-obama-s-numbers

Daly, T. (2019). *China's industrial slowdown and global supply chain shifts*. Reuters. Retrieved from https://www.reuters.com/article/china-economy-supply-chains/chinas-industrial-slowdown-and-global-supply-chain-shifts-idUSL4N29B3GJ

Haddad, B. (2018). The impact of drone strikes on civilian populations and regional stability. Journal of Conflict Studies, 39(2), 215-233.

Investopedia. (n.d.). *Tariffs are hitting the economy where it hurts*. Retrieved from https://www.investopedia.com/tariffs-are-hitting-the-economy-where-it-hurts-11705264

Lardy, N. R. (2020). *The state strikes back: The end of economic reform in China?* Brookings Institution Press.

Law & Crime. (2020). *Was Trump Admin Killing of Qassem Soleimani Legal?*. Retrieved from https://lawandcrime.com/legal-analysis/the-trump-admins-likely-legal-justifications-for-bypassing-congress-to-kill-qassem-soleimani/

Lee, M. (2021). *China's Belt and Road Initiative and global trade realignment*. International Journal of Economic Studies, 48(2), 112-134. Retrieved from https://www.ijes.org/articles/chinas-belt-and-road-initiative-and-global-trade-realignment

Lee, M. (2021). *Cyber threats and global supply chain vulnerabilities*. Journal of International Security Studies, 45(3), 78-95. Retrieved from https://www.jiss.org/articles/cyber-threats-and-global-supply-chain-vulnerabilities

Maguire, E. R., Nix, J., & Campbell, B. A. (2021). De-policing in the wake of the George Floyd protests: Exploring police disengagement and its impact on crime. Policing: An International Journal, 44(3), 452-468.

New York Magazine. (2019). *Trump's tariffs and the risk of recession*. Retrieved from https://nymag.com/intelligencer/article/trump-tariffs-effects-economy-recession-expert-predictions.html

Rosenfeld, R., Abt, T., & Lopez, E. (2021). Pandemic, social unrest, and crime in U.S. cities: 2020 year-end update. Council on Criminal Justice. Retrieved from https://counciloncj.org/pandemic-social-unrest-and-crime-in-us-cities-year-end-update/

Small Arms Survey. (2021). Global firearm ownership and gun sales surge in 2020. Retrieved from https://www.smallarmssurvey.org/database

United Nations. (2022). Global migration and the impact of U.S. immigration policies on refugee trends. Retrieved from https://www.un.org/migration-data

U.S. Department of Agriculture. (2021). *The impact of retaliatory tariffs on U.S. agriculture: 2018-2019*. Retrieved from https://ers.usda.gov/sites/default/files/_laserfiche/publications/102980/ERR-304.pdf

White House. (2021). Biden's statement on the Afghanistan withdrawal and its challenges. Retrieved from https://www.whitehouse.gov/statements-releases/2021/08/31/biden-addresses-afghanistan-withdrawal

PART 4: RECLAIMING THE NARRATIVE—HOW DEMOCRATS CAN WIN IN A MAGA WORLD

Chapter 13: A Better Vision for America

Brennan Center for Justice. (2023). Voting rights and election integrity in the United States: Challenges and reforms. Retrieved from https://www.brennancenter.org/our-work/research-reports/voting-rights-and-election-integrity

Brookings Institution. (2022). How economic inequality affects political polarization in the U.S. Retrieved from https://www.brookings.edu/articles/how-economic-inequality-affects-political-polarization-in-the-us/

Center for American Progress. (2022). Progressive taxation and economic justice: Ensuring fair wealth distribution. Retrieved from https://www.americanprogress.org/article/progressive-taxation-and-economic-justice

Congressional Research Service. (2022). *The Corporate Minimum Tax and Its Potential Effects.* Retrieved from https://crsreports.congress.gov/

Economic Policy Institute. (2021). Raising the minimum wage: Effects on workers, businesses, and the economy. Retrieved from https://www.epi.org/publication/raising-the-minimum-wage-effects-on-workers-businesses-and-the-economy

Economic Policy Institute. (2023). The state of working America wages 2023: Wage growth and inequality trends. Retrieved from https://www.epi.org/publication/the-state-of-working-america-wages-2023

Inequality.org. (2025). *Raising Capital Gains Taxes Would Reduce Inequality Without Economic Costs.* Retrieved from https://inequality.org/article/capital-gains-taxes-inequality/

Internal Revenue Service. (n.d.). *Corporate Alternative Minimum Tax.* Retrieved from https://www.irs.gov/inflation-reduction-act-of-2022/corporate-alternative-minimum-tax

Judis, J. B., & Teixeira, R. (2023). *Where have all the Democrats gone? The soul of the party in the age of extremes*. St. Martin's Press.

National Law Review. (2022). *Understanding the Corporate Minimum Tax Under the Inflation Reduction Act*. Retrieved from https://www.natlawreview.com/article/corporate-minimum-tax-inflation-reduction-act

National Women's Law Center. (2023). The economic impact of reproductive rights restrictions on women and families. Retrieved from https://nwlc.org/resource/economic-impact-of-reproductive-rights-restrictions

Pew Research Center. (2022). Partisan divides on LGBTQ+ rights, gender equality, and social justice issues. Retrieved from https://www.pewresearch.org/social-trends/2022/partisan-divides-on-lgbtq-rights-gender-equality-and-social-justice

Pew Research Center. (2023). Americans' views on identity politics and economic policy. Retrieved from https://www.pewresearch.org/politics/2023/americans-views-on-identity-politics-and-economic-policy

Urban Institute. (2022). The impact of infrastructure investment on job creation and economic growth. Retrieved from https://www.urban.org/research/publication/impact-infrastructure-investment-job-creation-and-economic-growth

White House. (2021). The Bipartisan Infrastructure Law: Investing in America's future. Retrieved from https://www.whitehouse.gov/briefing-room/statements-releases/2021/11/15/the-bipartisan-infrastructure-law-investing-in-americas-future

Chapter 14: Fighting Misinformation and Engaging with MAGA Supporters

Allcott, H., & Gentzkow, M. (2017). Social media and fake news in the 2016 election. Journal of Economic Perspectives, 31(2), 211–236. Retrieved from https://doi.org/10.1257/jep.31.2.211

Brennan Center for Justice. (2023). Voting rights and election integrity in the United States: Challenges and reforms. Retrieved from https://www.brennancenter.org/our-work/research-reports/voting-rights-and-election-integrity

Brookings Institution. (2023). How misinformation threatens democracy and what can be done about it. Retrieved from https://www.brookings.edu/articles/how-misinformation-threatens-democracy-and-what-can-be-done-about-it

Fukuyama, F. (2020). The demand for dignity and the politics of resentment. Journal of Democracy, 31(1), 5–17. Retrieved from https://doi.org/10.1353/jod.2020.0000

Ipsos. (2021). Public trust in elections and democratic institutions. Retrieved from https://www.ipsos.com/en-us/news-polls/public-trust-elections-2021

Pew Research Center. (2022). The role of social media in political polarization and misinformation. Retrieved from https://www.pewresearch.org/politics/2022/the-role-of-social-media-in-political-polarization-and-misinformation

PolitiFact. (2023). Fact-checking claims about the 2020 election and voter fraud. Retrieved from https://www.politifact.com/article/2023/fact-checking-claims-about-the-2020-election-and-voter-fraud/

Tucker, J. A., Guess, A., Barbera, P., Vaccari, C., Siegel, A., Sanovich, S., Stukal, D., & Nyhan, B. (2018). Social media, political polarization, and political disinformation: A review of the scientific literature. Political Science Research and Methods, 7(3), 201–230. Retrieved from https://doi.org/10.1017/psrm.2018.23

Vosoughi, S., Roy, D., & Aral, S. (2018). The spread of true and false news online. Science, 359(6380), 1146–1151. Retrieved from https://doi.org/10.1126/science.aap9559

White House. (2022). Efforts to combat misinformation and strengthen democracy. Retrieved from https://www.whitehouse.gov/briefing-room/statements-releases/2022/06/14/efforts-to-combat-misinformation-and-strengthen-democracy

About the author

Justin T. Hileman is a data-driven political analyst, writer, and advocate for media literacy whose work bridges the worlds of statistics, public policy, and civic engagement. Currently, he serves as a Sales Operations Analyst and as a Junior Biostatistician, applying rigorous statistical methods to improve decision-making in both healthcare and operations.

Justin's path to political writing started at home, where curiosity, open debate, and a sense of civic duty were part of everyday life. He grew up surrounded by conversations that weren't about pushing one ideology but about digging for the truth. That early exposure sparked a lasting interest in how stories shape the way people see politics and policy. He began college at the U.S. Air Force Academy, where he learned the value of leadership and service. But over time, he realized his real passion was understanding how misinformation spreads and how public trust is built—or broken. So, he shifted gears and earned a B.S. in Statistics from the University of Florida, then studied Applied Statistics in graduate school at Colorado State University.

That background in data analysis shapes how he sees politics. As Justin puts it, *"We never truly 'accept' a hypothesis; we only fail to reject it."* That mindset—grounded in humility and evidence—runs through everything he writes. It's also the heart of his first book, *MAGA in Context: The*

Rise, Rhetoric, and Reality of a Movement. Instead of just fact-checking or calling out lies, the book focuses on what's often left out: the missing context that can change how facts are understood. Justin's aim isn't just to correct the record but to reshape the whole conversation.

Professionally, Justin has co-led statistical analyses that support healthcare quality improvement, designed operational dashboards for supply chain optimization, and contributed to research on patient outcomes. These experiences shaped his ability to translate complex data into actionable insights, a skill he brings to his political analysis and writing. Through countless discussions with academic peers and friends, he has learned to challenge his assumptions, support his views with data, and communicate complex issues with clarity and humility.

His bigger mission is to help readers think more critically, ask better questions, and engage more honestly with the issues that matter most. He plans to keep writing, push for stronger media literacy, and eventually step into public service—bringing a transparent, data-driven voice to politics. For Justin, *MAGA in Context* is not just a critique- it is an invitation for readers to seek clarity in a world often clouded by confusion and to believe that democracy thrives only when the public is well-informed and willing to ask better questions.

Justin writes not to assert final answers but to pursue the most honest, well-rounded perspective possible, grounded in humility, clarity, and intellectual honesty. His work reflects the belief that reclaiming context is essential for a healthier democracy and a more informed public.

www.ingramcontent.com/pod-product-compliance
Lightning Source LLC
Chambersburg PA
CBHW070616030426
42337CB00020B/3817